Lift

AUTHORS

Kate Adams

Sarah Worthington

PROGRAM ADVISOR

Nonie K. Lesaux

NATIONAL GEOGRAPHIC
LEARNING

Australia · Brazil · Canada · Mexico · Singapore · United Kingdom · United States

NATIONAL GEOGRAPHIC LEARNING

National Geographic Learning,
a Cengage Company

Lift Fundamentals Student's Book
Authors: Kate Adams, Sarah Worthington

Publishers: Erik Gundersen, Janine Boylan

Managing Editor: Nancy Jordan

Senior Development Editor: Eve Einselen Yu

Director of Global Marketing: Ian Martin

Heads of Regional Marketing:

  Charlotte Ellis (Europe, Middle East and Africa)

  Justin Kaley (Asia and Greater China)

  Irina Pereyra (Latin America)

Product Marketing Manager: Anders Bylund

Senior Content Project Manager: Nick Ventullo

Media Researcher: Leila Hishmeh

Art Director: Brenda Carmichael

Operations Support: Hayley Chwazik-Gee

Manufacturing Planner: Mary Beth Hennebury

Composition: MPS North America, LLC

For permission to use material from this text or product, submit all requests online at **cengage.com/permissions** Further permissions questions can be emailed to **permissionrequest@cengage.com**

Student's Book ISBN: 978-0-357-50112-2

Student's Book + Sticker Code ISBN: 978-0-357-50116-0

National Geographic Learning
200 Pier 4 Boulevard
Boston, MA 02210
USA

Locate your local office at **international.cengage.com/region**

Visit National Geographic Learning online at **ELTNGL.com**
Visit our corporate website at **www.cengage.com**

Printed in Mexico
Print Number: 01 Print Year: 2021

PROGRAM ADVISOR

Nonie K. Lesaux, Harvard Graduate School of Education

ADVISORS

Emily Phillips Galloway, Assistant Professor, School of Education, Vanderbilt University's Peabody College

Margo Gottlieb, Co-Founder and Lead Developer, WIDA

Helyn Kim, Education Research Analyst, Institute of Education Sciences

Alexis Menten, Managing Director, Center for Global Education, Asia Society

Heather Michael, Citadel High School International Baccalaureate Coordinator, Halifax

Silvana Richardson, Head of Education, Bell English

REVIEWERS

ASIA

Tim Allen, Shenzhen RDF International School, Shenzhen

Lindsey Devillier, Beijing World Youth Academy, Beijing

Rivers He, Houhai English, Beijing

William Phillips, Aga Khan Education Service Central Asia, Tajikistan

Alex Shen, Phoenix International School, Guangzhou

Jonathan Tragash, Huamei Experimental School, Guangzhou International School, Guangzhou

Erin Volkert, Beijing World Youth Academy, Beijing

Dongjing Wang, Whales English, Beijing

Yan Zhou, Hangzhou Yungu School, Hangzhou

MIDDLE EAST

Adwoa Appiah-Boateng, ADNOC Schools, Abu Dhabi, United Arab Emirates

Diana Al-Mokdad, Sharjah American International School, Sharjah, United Arab Emirates

Khaled Qattawi, King Faisal School, Riyadh, Saudi Arabia

LATIN AMERICA

Kelli Brown, Modern Academy Cancun, Cancun, Mexico

Edith Guay, Sendica Education, Monterrey, Mexico

Verónica Malpica, Colegio Santa Engracia, Monterrey, Mexico

Dana Pao, Colegio Rochester, Bogotá, Colombia

Fernando Soler, Gimnasio Fontana, Bogotá, Colombia

EUROPE

Dr. Jana Pridalova, Lyceum Alpinum Zuoz AG, Zuoz, Switzerland

Julia Shewry, St. John's International School, Waterloo, Belgium

UNITED STATES

Connie Banks, Greenville Spartanburg Public Schools, Greenville, South Carolina

Barbara Brimmerman, Omaha Public Schools, Omaha, Nebraska

Maya Stewart, DC International School, Washington, DC

CONTENTS AT A GLANCE

☐ = National Geographic Exclusive

1 Empathy

Why is empathy important?

2 Problem Solving

What problems can young people solve?

3 Perspective

Why do people see the same things differently?

READING 1
p. 90

The Boy and the Whale
by Mordicai Gerstein

READING STRATEGY:
Describe a Story's Plot

GRAMMAR:
Prepositions of Place
and Direction

UNCOVER THE STORY
p. 100

FINE ART
by Ai-Da

READING 2
p. 102

The Subway Experiment
by Katherine Catmull

VOCABULARY:
Prefixes That Mean *Not*

READING SKILL:
Identify the Central Idea of a Text

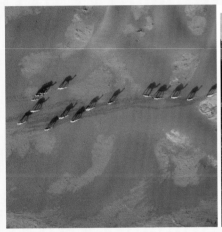

4 Language

What effect can words have?

5 Determination

What makes someone determined?

6 Becoming Me

ESSENTIAL QUESTION

How do I become who I want to be?

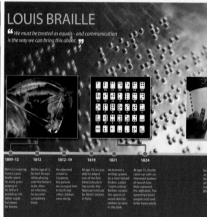

READING 1
p. 202

from **Rickshaw Girl**
by Mitali Perkins

READING STRATEGY:
Make Text-to-Self Connections

GRAMMAR:
Possessive Nouns and Adjectives

UNCOVER THE STORY
p. 214

INFOGRAPHIC:
Louis Braille

READING 2
p. 216

**Amalia Hernández:
A Dancer's Dream**
by Jane Skinner

VOCABULARY STRATEGY:
Use a Dictionary

READING SKILL:
Analyze Events

7 Nature

ESSENTIAL QUESTION
How does nature affect us?

8 Designing Our World

How should we design our world?

GENRES AT A GLANCE

NONFICTION

1 Empathy

"*Be a rainbow in someone else's cloud.*"

—MAYA ANGELOU,
AMERICAN POET

What does this quote mean to you?

Look at the photo and caption. Discuss the questions.

1. How are the window washers dressed, and why do you think they are dressed this way?

2. How does the little boy seem to react? Who benefits from this act of kindness?

◀ **At a children's hospital in São Paulo, Brazil, two window washers dressed up as superheroes and entertained sick children.**

3

ESSENTIAL QUESTION
Why is empathy important?

Theme Vocabulary

Use these words to express your ideas throughout the unit.

PRACTICE 1 Read the conversation. Think about the meaning of each word in **bold**. Then write each word next to its definition in the chart below.

> When you see a new student at school, what do you do?

> I always say "Hi" to new students. But sometimes some people **treat** new students **badly**. For example, they don't sit next to the new students at lunch or talk to them in class. I **imagine** that doesn't feel good. I try to have **empathy**. It's not easy to go to a new school. I hope my actions have a good **impact** on their day. I hope they feel better.

Theme Vocabulary

badly (adv.)
empathy (n.)
imagine (v.)
impact (n.)
treat (v.)

Word	Definition
badly	in bad manner or way
	an effect; a change caused by some action or event
	to think or create in your mind
	the feeling that you understand and share another person's feelings
	to think and act toward someone in a specific way

PRACTICE 2 Work with a partner. Answer the questions about the conversation.

1. How does the student show empathy?
2. Why does the student show empathy?

Explore the Essential Question

Think What is empathy? How do you show it? Circle your answer. Then use this key to find your total score:

always = 3, almost always = 2, sometimes = 1, never = 0

Do you have empathy?

_____ When someone is talking to me, I listen. I do not interrupt.

    always   almost always   sometimes   never

_____ When my friend is happy, I feel happy, too.

    always   almost always   sometimes   never

_____ When I'm with other people, I look at their faces to understand their feelings.

    always   almost always   sometimes   never

_____ When I'm with someone who is different from me, I try to find something similar between us.

    always   almost always   sometimes   never

_____ When I see people who are sad, I want to help them.

    always   almost always   sometimes   never

Total Score _____

Discuss Write another sentence to add to the quiz. Share your new sentence with a partner. Then add points to your score.

_____

Respond Circle the words related to *empathy*. Then use some of the words to complete the sentences below. Share your ideas with a partner.

imagine   respond   connect   help

kind   listen   empathy   think of others

nice   caring   friendly   talk   feelings

understand   feel better

People show empathy when they _____.

People who show empathy are _____.

Key Vocabulary

PRACTICE Look at the photos and read the sentences. Discuss the meaning of the words in **bold** with a partner. Then ask and answer the questions.

alone (adjective)
This student is **alone**.
When is it good to be alone?

artist (noun)
An **artist** creates art, such as paintings.
Do you have a friend who is an artist?

awkward (adjective)
This student feels **awkward**.
What situations can make someone feel awkward?

cool (adjective)
These students are **cool**. Other students really like them.
What do you think makes someone cool?

presentation (noun)
This student is giving a **presentation**.
Do you like giving presentations? Explain.

volunteer (verb)
Lily **volunteered** to answer the question.
How often do you volunteer to speak in class?

Grammar: Simple Present Tense and Present Progressive

Simple Present Tense

We often use the **simple present tense** to talk about facts, daily activities, opinions, and habits. The third-person singular form always ends in -*s*.

*Baseball **is** a sport.* (fact)

*They **attend** high school.* (daily activity)

*Baseball **looks** fun.* (opinion)

*He **draws** cartoons.* (habit)

PRACTICE 1 Complete the sentences with the simple present form of the verb in parentheses.

1. Sunspots _____ (be) dark spots on the sun.

2. Scientists _____ (look) for new sunspots regularly.

3. When a sunspot _____ (appear) on the sun's surface, a scientist _____ (draw) it.

4. After days or weeks, the sunspot _____ (disappear).

◁ A large sunspot is seen on the surface of the sun during a partial eclipse.

Present Progressive

The **present progressive** is used for actions that are happening at the moment of speaking or will happen soon. The present progressive is formed with the correct form of the verb *be* and the present participle (-*ing*) form of the main verb.

*I **am studying** for my math test.*

*We **are starting** our group presentations today.*

PRACTICE 2 Read the paragraph. Complete the sentences with the present progressive form of the verb in parentheses.

    The students _____ (work) on presentations in English class. Some students in the class _____ (plan) their presentations. They _____ (talk) about their topics. Other students _____ (take) notes. Jensen _____ (draw) pictures of baseball players. Jorge _____ (write) about the history of baseball.

ESSENTIAL QUESTION

Why is empathy important?

First Thoughts

What is happening in these frames? How does each boy feel? Write your ideas below. Then discuss them with a partner.

Discuss Read the sentences. Check (✓) the sentences that show empathy. Then discuss the questions below with a partner.

☐ He doesn't know about baseball? Cool. I can teach him about it!

☐ So awkward! I hope he says something.

☐ Maybe I can find out what he likes. We can talk about what he likes.

☐ I can't do a presentation with someone who doesn't talk.

☐ Sometimes I like to work alone. Maybe he wants to work alone.

1. What do you think when you meet someone shy or different from you?

2. What are some other ways to show empathy for someone who is shy or different from you?

Reading Strategy: Monitor Understanding

When you **monitor understanding**, you make sure you understand the text you are reading. Good readers think about what they do and don't understand as they read. To monitor understanding, follow these steps:

1. Pause after each paragraph or section you read. Ask yourself: *Does this make sense? Are there any words I don't know? What happened? Has this ever happened to me?*

2. If you are having trouble understanding, stop reading.

3. Choose one of these strategies to fix the problem.

   - Reread the sentence, paragraph, or section.
   - If the problem is a word or phrase, see if another word or phrase works instead.
   - Read the next sentence or paragraph.
   - Look at any visuals in the text.
   - Make a connection to something in your life.

Strategy in Action

Read the frames from "That Sports Dude" from *Brave* and a reader's thoughts. What problem did the reader have? With a partner, say which strategies the reader used to fix the problem. Then discuss what "hammering out" means.

The teacher wants students to start "writing" or "discussing" a task.

I don't know the phrase "hammering out." I will reread the sentence. I can also think about other words that work instead.

I know a hammer is a tool used to pound nails. You hit them hard many times. I know it can be hard work!

I can read ahead and look at the visuals. I see lots of talking. I think "hammering out" means "to discuss and work through something."

Read and answer the questions: **What is Jensen good at? What is difficult for him?**
As you read, underline any parts of the text you have questions about or find confusing.

That Sports Dude

from **Brave**

by **Svetlana Chmakova**

HEY, MATT! YOU, ME—GROUP?

OKAY.

MELISSA, YOU'RE IN MINE!

UH.

UM.

THERE'S... NO ONE ELSE I CAN ASK.

DO YOU HAVE A GROUP, JENSEN?

UH... N-NO...

OKAY, WHO'S GOT ROOM FOR JENSEN?

STOP & THINK
Interpret What does "Who's got room for Jensen?" mean?

UH... NOT US!

WE'VE ALREADY GOT THREE.

US TOO.

I COULD... JUST BE MY OWN GROUP.

ALL RIGHT, I NEED A VOLUNTEER TO LEAVE THEIR GROUP TO BE JENSEN'S PARTNER!

I'LL DO IT, MISS LEE.

GREAT! THANK YOU, JORGE!

NOW, EACH GROUP WILL PICK A PRESENTATION TOPIC[1] WHILE I HAND OUT THE GUIDELINES.

...

STOP & THINK
Explain Why does the author include "yammer" and "chatter" in the background of this frame?

YAMMER CHATTE HA HA

BASEBALL.

H-HUH?

FOR THE TOPIC?

...O-OH!

Y-YEAH, OKAY.

...

...

...

---

[1] **topic** subject

...ANYWAY!

DID YOU GUYS SEE THAT NEW TRAILER[2] FOR STAR WARS?

OH! IS IT OUT?

...THIS IS SO AWKWARD.

RRRING

...BUT, YAY, ENGLISH IS NEXT! I'M SO GLAD I HAVE A PARTNER FOR THAT PRESENTATION.

BASEBALL.

...EVEN IF IT'S THAT SPORTS DUDE, JORGE.

STOP & THINK
Deduce Why does Jensen describe Jorge as "that sports dude"?

CLICK

HE VOLUNTEERED TO BE IN A GROUP WITH ME...

NO ONE DOES THAT!

[2] **trailer** movie advertisement

...HE LOOKS LIKE HE COULD STOP AN ENTIRE BASEBALL TEAM. BY HIMSELF.

...

THAT WAS THE BELL, JORGE. CAN YOU PUT THAT PHONE AWAY?

YES.

SORRY, MISS LEE.

....!

OKAY, EVERYONE, TODAY IS A WORK PERIOD FOR YOUR PRESENTATIONS!

OH NO!!

...THE BASEBALL BOOK!

I COMPLETELY FORGOT TO EVEN FLIP THROUGH IT!

I WANT YOU TO START HAMMERING OUT YOUR SUBTOPICS AND OUTLINE.

I'LL BE WALKING AROUND AND ANSWERING ANY QUESTIONS.

STOP & THINK
Restate What subtopic do Jorge and Jensen choose?

[3] **into** interested in

STOP & THINK
Describe How do the two boys in the lunchroom treat Jensen?

[4] **neighborhood watch** a community program to keep people safe

© 2017 Svetlana Chmakova. First published by Yen Press, LLC, New York, NY

STOP & THINK
Interpret What do you think Jorge means by telling Sean to "dial it back to civil"?

⁵ **weasel** sneaky
⁶ **dial it back** reduce it or make it less extreme

STOP & THINK
Describe How do Jorge and his friends treat Jensen at lunch? How do you know?

ENGLISH CLASS
(WORK PERIOD AT THE LIBRARY.)

GLOOM

...

...

...

DUDE,
DID YOUR
DOG DIE OR
SOMETHING?

STOP & THINK
Restate What does Jorge mean when he asks, "did your dog die or something"?

...

I-I...

I'M FAILING MATH...

...AND...I HAVE TO...

...GO TO A...

...A TUTORING GROUP...

...INSTEAD OF ART CLUB...

AH.

...

BUMMER.

...TUTORING'S
GOOD THOUGH.

I GOT SOME FOR SCIENCE.
REALLY SAVED ME.

R-REALLY?

YEAH.
THAT STUFF, LIKE,
MAKES SENSE[7] NOW.

HUH! MAYBE IT
WON'T BE SO BAD.

...

THOUGH,
I'LL STILL BE
MISSING ART
CLUB...

I'M WORRIED MY
ART FRIENDS MIGHT
FORGET ABOUT ME...
AGAIN...

© 2017 Svetlana Chmakova. First published by Yen Press, LLC, New York, NY

---

[7] **makes sense** is easy to understand

...THEY FORGET
ABOUT YOU?

...THOSE DON'T
SOUND LIKE FRIENDS.

NO, NO, IT'S NOT LIKE
THAT! THEY'RE JUST...
BUSY. LOTS TO DO...

...

...IF THEY'RE
FRIENDS, THEN THEY'VE
GOT YOUR BACK[8]...

...WHETHER YOU'RE
THERE OR NOT.

...

FRIENDS WON'T "FORGET"
ABOUT YOU.

...OH.

STOP & THINK
Contrast Jensen
thinks the kids in Art
Club are his friends.
What does Jorge
think?

RRING

JORGE IS SO COOL.

LATER.

BYE!

---

[8] **they've got your back** they treat you well

© 2017 Svetlana Chmakova. First published by Yen Press, LLC, New York, NY

9 **'sup** short for *What's up?*, meaning "How are you?" (slang)
10 **in charge of** responsible for

About the Author

Svetlana Chmakova has written many manga, graphic novels, and comic books. She also draws the illustrations. She moved from Russia to Canada when she was sixteen years old.

---

[11] **on point** just right, very good

Close Read

Work with a partner.

1. Determine the meanings of your underlined words and phrases.
2. Discuss the questions:

    What is Jensen good at? What is difficult for him?

Understand

Complete the summary below with the words in the box:

badly	likes	making	nice	presentation	volunteers	writing

Jensen doesn't have a partner for his project in English class. Jorge _____ to be his partner. They have to give a _____. They decide to write about the impact of baseball on American culture. At lunch, two boys treat Jensen _____. Jorge and his friends join Jensen and scare the boys. Jorge's friends are _____ to Jensen. In English class, Jorge is _____ the presentation while Jensen is _____ the visuals. Jorge _____ Jensen's drawings.

Read Again and Analyze

Read the story again and respond to the questions. Use evidence from the text to support your responses.

1. **Characterize** How would you describe Jorge?
2. **Infer** Why does Jorge volunteer to be Jensen's partner in English class?
3. **Contrast** How does Jensen feel about his English presentation at the beginning of the story? How does he feel at the end?
4. **Deduce** What impact do Jorge's words and actions have on Jensen?

Apply the Strategy: Monitor Understanding

Identify a section of the story that you did not understand. Check (✓) the strategies you used to fix the problem. Write what you learned from each strategy you used.

I didn't understand _____ on page # _____.

✓	Strategy	What I Learned
	Reread a sentence or paragraph.	
	See if another word or phrase works.	
	Read ahead a sentence or paragraph.	
	Look at the visuals from the text.	
	Make a connection to something in your life.	

Share Your Perspective

Discuss the questions in a small group.

1. Are Jorge and Jensen friends?
2. How should you treat your classmates? Do you need to be friends with everyone?
3. What are you good at? Who in your class is especially good at something (e.g., drawing, writing, singing, or dancing)?

Discussion Frames

I think/don't think …

In my opinion, classmates should treat each other …

I am pretty good at … My friend … is very good at

Reflect

How does "That Sports Dude" from *Brave* help you understand why empathy is important? With a partner, use some of the words to write sentences about the story.

Nouns	Verbs	Adjectives / Adverbs
artists empathy impact presentation	imagine treat volunteer	alone awkward badly cool

_____

_____

_____

Examine the Photo

1. Look at the photo. Describe what you see.

2. Why do you think the people in the photo are happy? Give evidence to support your opinion.

3. Write 3 questions about the photo. Discuss your questions with a small group.

Find Out ▶ 1.1

Watch photographer Brent Stirton talk about his photo.

1. Did he answer any of your questions? Which ones?

2. According to Brent, why are the people in the photo happy? Tell Anita's story.

3. How is Anita's life different now?

4. Why is this photo about empathy?

Reflect

Imagine you are a child from Anita's school and it is before her life changed. How can you be kind to her? Write three ideas.

Share Your Story

1. Take or find a photo that shows a happy scene. What story does the photo tell? How does looking at the photo make you feel?

2. Tell your classmates the story. Describe the impact the photo has on you.

ABOUT THE PHOTOGRAPHER

Brent Stirton's photographs tell stories. He wants to inspire people to help others and to protect nature.

Key Vocabulary

PRACTICE Look at the photos and read the sentences. Discuss the meaning of the words in **bold** with a partner. Then ask and answer the questions.

bother (verb)
There was a lot of noise in the room, and it **bothered** her.
What bothers you?

miserable (adjective)
His team lost the game. He feels **miserable**.
How can people feel better when they are miserable?

pay attention (verb phrase)
I **pay attention** to my teacher.
How do you know when someone is paying attention to you?

seem (verb)
He **seems** very happy.
When a friend seems happy, what do you do?

surprising (adjective)
The ending of the show was **surprising**.
What movie or story has a surprising ending?

unkind (adjective)
She received an **unkind** message.
How do you feel when someone is unkind?

Vocabulary: Use Context Clues to Understand Meaning

When you don't understand a word or phrase in a text, look for **context clues**, or the words and sentences around it. To use context clues to understand a word or phrase, follow these steps:

1. Look for words that connect ideas in the text.
   - *And* connects similar ideas. (*unhappy* **and** *sad*)
   - *But* connects different ideas. (*tired* **but** *happy*)
   - *Or* connects a similar word or phrase. (*to be mean* **or** *to say something unkind*)

2. Look for examples and descriptions. Examples may begin with the words *for example* or *for instance*.

3. Guess the meaning of the word or phrase from the context.

4. Reread the text again to check your new understanding. Use a dictionary if you are still unsure.

Examples:

Some young people aren't very nice to their brothers and sisters or to their classmates at school. <u>They call them names</u>, <u>pick on them</u>, <u>or try to ruin their fun</u>. They might pretend to be your friend and then say very unkind things behind your back. It seems like all they want is for other people to feel <u>small **and** stupid</u>.

> I don't know what *pick on* means. I'll look at the words and sentences around it. I see the words "or try to ruin their fun." I also see "They call them names." All of this describes how people aren't very nice. I think *pick on* means "to be mean to someone."

> I don't understand the word *small* in this paragraph. I see the words "and stupid." After I reread, I think *small* is a negative word like *stupid*. I think "to feel small" is to feel bad about yourself.

PRACTICE Read the excerpt from the text you will read, and write answers to the questions below.

People who are actually strong and confident are almost always gentle and kind to others. If someone is mean, it may be because at home, or in the past, something or someone has frightened them. Maybe they have an older brother who picks on them.

1. What word helps you understand the meaning of *confident*? _____
2. What word helps you understand the meaning of *gentle*? _____
3. What example helps you understand *frightened*? _____
4. What do you think *frightened* means? _____

ESSENTIAL QUESTION

Why is empathy important?

First Thoughts

1. What is the boy in the middle doing? What are the other students doing? Tell a partner your ideas.

2. With a partner, write three sentences to tell a story based on the photo.

_____

_____

_____

3. Write a title for the picture. _____

Discuss Read the sentences. Place an **✗** on the line to show how strongly you agree or disagree. Then compare and discuss with a partner.

	Strongly Disagree	Not Sure	Strongly Agree
1. People who are happy usually treat others with kindness.	←———————————————→		
2. People who are miserable often act like they are happy.	←———————————————→		
3. People are mean because they feel bad about themselves.	←———————————————→		
4. I can understand why someone treats another person badly.	←———————————————→		
5. Most people have been hurt by someone's unkind words.	←———————————————→		

Reading Strategy: Paraphrase

When you **paraphrase**, you put someone's ideas in your own words. Good readers paraphrase sentences from the text to check their understanding. To paraphrase when you read, follow these steps:

1. After you read a few sentences, ask yourself: *What is the author saying? How can I explain these ideas to someone else?* Reread the text. Make sure you understand.

2. Paraphrase the ideas. Use your own words to say the same ideas. Try to use fewer words than the text.

3. Reread the text. Check that your paraphrase expresses the same ideas.

Strategy in Action

Read the paragraph from "People Are Unhappy, Not Mean" and a reader's thoughts. Look at how the student paraphrases the sentences from the text. Then with a partner, paraphrase the last sentence. Write your paraphrase below.

Some people treat others badly.

The person who is treated badly can feel very unhappy.

Some young people aren't very nice to their brothers and sisters or to their classmates at school. They call them names, pick on them, or try to ruin their fun. They might pretend to be your friend and then say very unkind things behind your back. It seems like all they want is for other people to feel small and stupid. It can be really upsetting and even frightening to be made fun of. But why are people mean? Why does one person want to make another person feel miserable? The answer is surprising: it is often because these people feel small and miserable inside of themselves.

Why do people say or do unkind things?

_____

_____

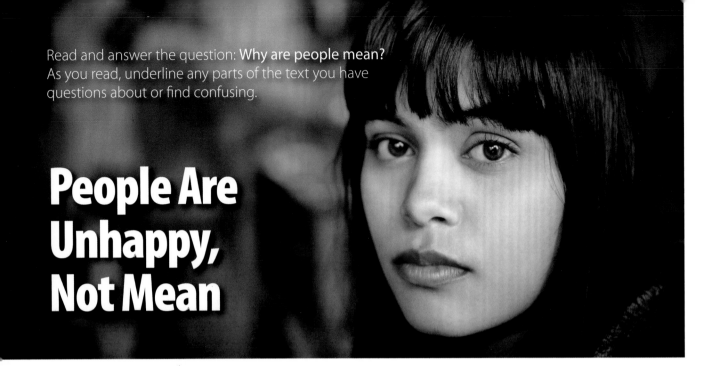

Read and answer the question: **Why are people mean?**
As you read, underline any parts of the text you have
questions about or find confusing.

People Are Unhappy, Not Mean

🎧 **1.2**

1   Some young people aren't very nice to their brothers and sisters
or to their classmates at school. They call them names, pick on them,
or try to ruin their fun. They might pretend to be your friend and then
say very **unkind** things behind your back.[1] It **seems** like all they want
5 is for other people to feel small and stupid. It can be really upsetting
and even frightening to be made fun of. But why are people mean?
Why does one person want to make another person feel **miserable**?

    The answer is **surprising**: it is often because these people
feel small and miserable inside of themselves. You wouldn't know
10 by looking at them—they might look strong and confident and
very pleased with themselves. They might seem to laugh a lot—
maybe at you.

    But if you think about it, no one who is really happy would
want to make another person unhappy. People who are actually
15 strong and confident are almost always gentle and kind to others.
If someone is mean, it may be because at home, or in the past,
something or someone has frightened them. Probably you'll never
know the details, but you can **imagine**. Maybe they have an older
brother who picks on them. Maybe their mom is always bossing
20 them about.[2] Maybe their parents shout at each other. Inside their
head, this person who seems so brave and fearless actually feels

> **STOP & THINK**
> **Explain** The author
> introduces examples
> with *Maybe*. What do
> these examples help
> you understand?

---

[1] **behind your back** without you knowing
[2] **bossing them about** telling them what to do in a mean way

sad and worried. They're too frightened to let anyone see how weak they really feel. As a result, they try to make themselves feel better by making another person suffer.[3]

25　　Those who have been hurt, hurt others. Understanding this does not immediately solve the problem if someone is being nasty to you, but it can help a little. It can help you to remember that you don't deserve to be **treated badly**. It's not something you've done. There isn't anything wrong with you. Think about a time when you haven't
30　been very nice to someone. Most people are a bit mean to someone at some point, or have wanted to be, even if they don't actually do or say anything. It's not bad or wrong. It's just life. Now think about why you were mean to that person. It's pretty much always because something else was **bothering** you, and you didn't know how to make it better.

35　　For instance, it is quite common for older children to get a bit nasty if there is a new baby in the family. Grown-ups think babies are very sweet. Everyone **pays attention** to them and says how cute they are. Parents spend all their time taking care of them. If you are a bit older and your parents have a new baby, it is not surprising
40　if you get angry. You might feel like people should be paying more attention to you. Maybe you want to show other people that you're also important. You want them to see that you are much better than this boring baby who everyone loves so much. So, you find someone who is weaker than you, and you start being mean to
45　them. It makes you feel powerful. It makes you feel better to know that someone else is feeling bad like you do. Of course, doing this isn't very nice, but it is understandable.[4] Sometimes when we are so sad and angry, there doesn't feel like anything else we can do. Realizing why you might not be very nice to other people can help
50　you see how someone else could be not very nice to you.

　　Understanding doesn't make everything suddenly perfect. If someone is being mean to you, the problem will not go away just because you understand that they may be unhappy inside. But when you understand things, they often stop being so frightening.
55　And that's a good start.

> **STOP & THINK**
> **Recognize** What is the example in this paragraph? What idea does it support?

---

[3] **suffer** feel miserable
[4] **understandable** normal

Close Read

Work with a partner.

1. Determine the meanings of your underlined words and phrases.

2. Discuss the question:

Why are people mean?

Apply the Strategy: Paraphrase

Discuss the meaning of the lines from the text with a partner. Then paraphrase them.

Text	Paraphrase
1. (Lines 25–29) Those who have been hurt, hurt others. Understanding this does not immediately solve the problem if someone is being nasty to you, but it can help a little. It can help you to remember that you don't deserve to be treated badly. It's not something you've done. There isn't anything wrong with you.	
2. (Lines 49–50) Realizing why you might not be very nice to other people can help you see how someone else could be not very nice to you.	
3. (Lines 51–54) Understanding doesn't make everything suddenly perfect. If someone is being mean to you, the problem will not go away just because you understand that they may be unhappy inside. But when you understand things, they often stop being so frightening.	

Understand

Do the sentences restate a main idea from the text? Check (✔) *Yes* or *No*. Then discuss your answers with a partner.

	Yes	No
1. People are often mean because they are suffering.	☐	☐
2. Unhappy people don't want to make others miserable.	☐	☐
3. Most people are frightened at some point in their life.	☐	☐
4. Pay attention to when you say unkind things. Then you can better understand why you and others say mean things.	☐	☐
5. Understanding why someone says something mean can help you feel less scared.	☐	☐

Read Again and Analyze

Read the text again and respond to the questions. Use evidence from the text to support your responses.

1. **Identify** Name three examples the author gives to explain why someone would be mean.

2. **Recognize** Does the author think that how we act matches how we feel on the inside? How do you know?

3. **Focus** Does the author think that it's normal to have mean thoughts? Why or why not?

4. **Examine** The author repeats important ideas. Find two places in the text where the author explains the same idea in different words.

5. **Infer** Why did the author write this article?

Share Your Perspective

Discuss the questions in a small group.

1. What does this article help you understand?

2. What are other reasons that people say unkind things?

3. If something is bothering you, what can you do so that you aren't unkind to someone else?

Discussion Frames

The article helps me understand …

In my opinion, people say unkind things because …

If something is bothering me, I can …

Reflect

How does "People Are Unhappy, Not Mean" help you understand empathy and why it is important? With a partner, use some of the words to write sentences about the text.

Nouns	Verbs and Verb Phrases	Adjectives and Adverbs
empathy impact	bother imagine pay attention seem treat	badly miserable surprising unkind

Advancing Conservation through Empathy for Wildlife

The zoo director interacts with a hippopotamus at Beauval Zoo in Saint-Aignan-sur-Cher, France.

First Thoughts

Imagine only one of these two animals can be protected in the wild. Which animal would you choose? With a partner, discuss why you chose that animal.

Viewing Skill: Predict

When you predict, you use what you already know and information from the video to guess what the video is about. This can help you if you do not understand every word. Look at the title and the images on the screen, and ask yourself what the purpose of the video is or what it is about.

Example: *I see the title "Advancing Conservation through Empathy for Wildlife." I think the video is trying to get people to care more about wildlife.*

Apply the Skill

▶ **1.2** Watch the video with the sound off. Write what you see. Use your notes to make predictions. Share your predictions with a partner.

I see …	I think …

Understand and Analyze

▶ **1.2** Watch again. Answer the questions. Support your responses with evidence from the video.

1. **Restate** What kind of organizations are involved in the project?
2. **Conclude** What is the goal of the project?
3. **Restate** What does it mean when the speaker says that "… emotions are an important driver towards conservation action"?
4. **Summarize** What do the speakers think will happen if people develop more empathy for animals?

Share Your Perspective

Discuss the questions in a small group.

1. What animals do you love and care about?
2. What activities should zoos include that would help people build empathy for animals?

Discussion Frames

I love …

Zoos should …

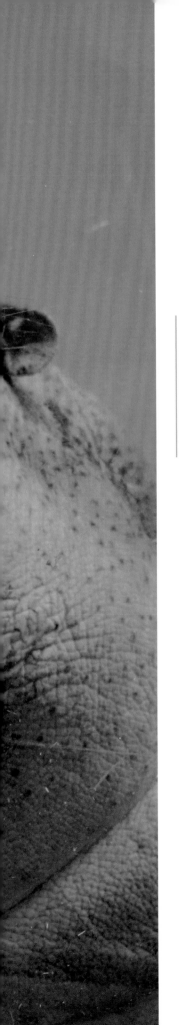

Reflect on the Essential Question

Think about the characters and people in this unit. What message does each give about empathy? Why is empathy important? Write your ideas in the idea web.

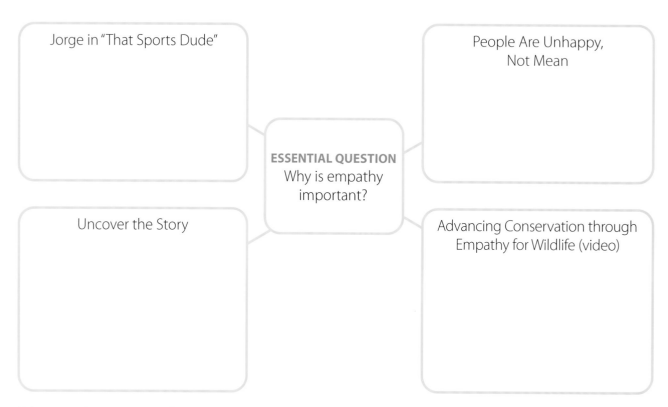

Jorge in "That Sports Dude"

People Are Unhappy, Not Mean

ESSENTIAL QUESTION
Why is empathy important?

Uncover the Story

Advancing Conservation through Empathy for Wildlife (video)

Discuss the Essential Question

Look at your ideas about the Essential Question earlier in the unit and your notes in the idea web above. How have your ideas about the Essential Question changed? What changed your ideas? Discuss your answers in a group.

Respond to the Essential Question

Write your response to the Essential Question.

Response Rubric	Theme Vocabulary
A good response will	**badly (adv.)**
✓ state your opinion	**empathy (n.)**
✓ provide support from the texts, the discussion, and your life	**imagine (v.)**
✓ use theme vocabulary	**impact (n.)**
	treat (v.)

Option 1: Compare Words and Pictures

The author of *Brave* sometimes uses drawings instead of words to show the characters' thoughts, actions, and feelings. She calls these drawings "visual tricks."

1. Find a frame in "That Sports Dude" from *Brave* where the picture tells you a lot about a character's thoughts, actions, or feelings.

2. Write sentences to explain what the picture shows.

3. Tell your partner which page the picture is on. Read your text. Can your partner guess which frame you are describing?

4. Discuss which you think works better, your words or the picture. Why?

Example:

This frame is on page 20. Jorge's friend Sean has just pushed the mean kid and told him to sit. The kid sits back down. Jensen is surprised and confused. He doesn't say anything. Jorge tells Sean to be civil, or polite.

Option 2: Create a Comic Strip

The author of "People Are Unhappy, Not Mean" asks readers to imagine why a person would be mean. With a group, create a comic strip about Yanik or Foster in "That Sports Dude" from *Brave*.

1. Discuss why the character treats Jensen badly. Create a story to explain.

2. Take notes in the chart to plan your comic strip.

3. Create 4–6 frames to tell the story. Write dialogue and draw images for the story.

4. Present your comic strip to the class.

	Description	Images
Who is the character?		
How is the character unkind?		
Why is he unkind?		
What happens?		
How does the character change?		

Assignment: Write about a Job that Requires Empathy

Descriptive writing describes a person, place, or thing. It creates a picture of the person, place, or thing in the reader's mind. In this assignment, you will write a **descriptive paragraph** about a job that requires empathy. Your paragraph should include:

- a title
- an introduction that describes the job
- a description of how someone doing the job has empathy
- details that help readers form pictures in their minds
- a photo of a person doing the job
- a caption to describe what the person is doing in the photo

Explore the Model

Read the model. How many sentences describe the empathy the person has? Which sentences are they?

Language for Writing

Read the model again.

1. Circle the simple present tense verbs in the model. Then underline the present progressive verbs in the caption.

2. List the verbs in the correct column. How do the descriptions of the verbs help you understand which tense to use?

Verbs that Describe the Job	Verbs that Describe the Photo

3. The writer uses *also* to share more examples about a similar idea. The word *also* comes after the verb *be*. Complete the sentence with the words from the model:

They are patient with animals that are nervous or shaking. Veterinarians _____ when they _____ .

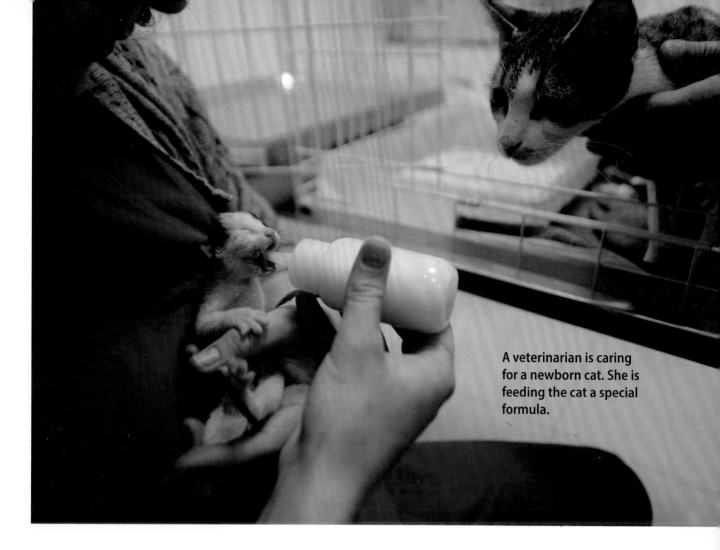

A veterinarian is caring for a newborn cat. She is feeding the cat a special formula.

Veterinarians Are Empathetic

The title and the introduction describe the job.

Veterinarians take care of sick animals. They have empathy for the owners and their animals. They are gentle with the animals. They move slowly and speak softly to the animals. They are patient with animals that are nervous or shaking. Veterinarians are also calm when they speak to the owners. They sometimes tell someone bad news about a pet. Empathy is a very important quality for veterinarians.

These sentences describe how someone doing the job has empathy. They use details that help me form a picture in my mind.

Plan Your Writing

Complete the outline.

- Choose a job that requires empathy. Write an introduction to describe the job.
- Write 2 or 3 sentences about how someone doing the job has empathy. Include details that help the readers form pictures in their minds.
- Find a photo of a person doing this job. Describe what is happening in the photo in a caption.
- Write a title.

Outline

Title:
A job that requires empathy:
Introduction that describes the job:
How someone doing the job has empathy: Sentence #1:   Sentence #2:   Sentence #3:
Photo or drawing of a person doing this job with a caption of what the person is doing:

Write and Revise

Write Use your outline to write a first draft.

- Use simple present and present progressive verbs correctly.
- Use *also* to give new examples.

Revise Exchange your descriptive paragraph with a partner. Using the checklist, review your partner's work and give feedback. Use feedback from your partner to revise your draft.

Feedback Frames

I like the details about …

In this sentence, you could add …

One question I have is …

- [ ] Does the introduction describe the job that requires empathy?

- [ ] Does the writer tell how someone doing the job has empathy?

- [ ] Does the writer include details that help readers form pictures in their minds?

- [ ] Does the writer include a photo?

- [ ] Does the writer describe the actions in the photo?

Proofread Check the grammar, spelling, punctuation, and capitalization in your paragraph. Make edits to correct any errors.

TIP

Check that you've used a capital letter at the beginning of each sentence and end punctuation at the end of each sentence. Check that you've used present simple and present progressive verb forms correctly.

Publish

Share your paragraph. Read two of your classmates' paragraphs.

Present Your Paragraph

You will present your paragraph about a job that requires empathy.

Look at the audience when you present. Look down at your notes only if you forget what to say.

Prepare to share your paragraph and photo:

- If you don't know how to pronounce a word, look it up or ask for help.
- Practice reading your paragraph to a partner.
- Speak slowly. Pause for a moment after each sentence.
- Point to the picture when you read the sentences about it.

Listen to others present their paragraphs.

- Listen to the presenter. Ask questions after the presentation.
- Give feedback. You can say, "I like the detail about …" or "I can tell that this person is …"

A family standing in front of their yurt in Mongolia.

Telling Stories with Photos 1.3

EXPLORER IN ACTION
Hannah Reyes Morales is a photographer and photojournalist.

Hannah Reyes Morales's love for photography started when she was a little girl. From her home in Manila, Philippines, photographs from *National Geographic* magazine were her "windows to the outside world." Through these photos, she saw new places. She imagined the lives of other people, and she felt connected to them.

Morales went on to take her own photos. By age 20, she was a photographer for newspapers. She now works as a photojournalist and is a National Geographic Explorer. Like the photos she saw in magazines as a girl, her photos have an impact. They tell a story. They often show people in difficult situations. But she shows them with empathy. Her photos invite the viewer to see the person and enter the person's story. They help people imagine the lives of others.

▶ **1.3** Answer the questions. Then watch the video to learn more.

1. Morales loved _____ as a young girl. They helped her to imagine _____ .

2. Now Morales is a _____ . Her photos show people _____ .

How Will You Take Action?

Choose one or more of these actions to do.

Personal

Be nice to yourself.

1. Notice your thoughts when you make a mistake. Are they kind or unkind?
2. Treat yourself as a friend. What can you say? Think of a kinder message.
3. Each day, notice your thoughts. Practice being kind to yourself.

School

Join or create a program at your school to welcome new students.

1. Create a list of activities for students to help new students feel welcome. For example, give a school tour, eat lunch together, or be a friend for the week and show the new student the daily routine.
2. Discuss ideas. Then create a plan to match new students with others and help welcome them to the school.

Local

Help people or animals in your community.

1. Identify people or animals in need in your community.
2. Join a community group or volunteer to help. For example, help prepare food for people or help take care of animals that don't have homes.
3. What impact can your actions have? How can you get more people to help?

Global

Make a friend across the world from you.

1. A pen pal is someone you write to in a different part of the world. You learn about your pen pal's life and you share about yours.
2. Work with your teacher to join a pen pal program. Learn about someone else. Imagine life in a different place. Share what you learn with your classmates.

Reflect

Reflect on your Take Action project(s). Then complete the sentences.

1. My project(s) was/were successful because

_____.

2. One thing I wish I had done differently is

_____.

3. Because of what I learned in this unit, one thing I will do is

_____.

2 Problem Solving

"When children and young people speak, the world should listen."

—**CHARLOTTE PETRI GORNITZKA, SWEDISH MANAGEMENT CONSULTANT**

What does this quote mean to you?

Look at the photo and caption. Discuss the questions.

1. What does the device Gitanjali Rao is holding in her hand do?

2. What problem did she want to help solve? Why do you think she wanted to help?

◄ **Eleven-year-old Gitanjali Rao learned about people getting sick from their drinking water and wanted to help. She designed a device called Tethys that measures lead levels in water.**

ESSENTIAL QUESTION

What problems can young people solve?

Theme Vocabulary

Use these words to express your ideas throughout the unit.

PRACTICE 1 Read the conversation. Think about the meaning of each word in **bold**. Then write each word next to its definition in the chart below.

> Can young people **solve** difficult problems?

> Yes. Young people are **creative**. They often think of new **ideas**. Also, they think about the future. For example, they **wonder** what climate change will do to the Earth. There are many examples of **youth** finding **solutions** in the past, too. In 1824, Louis Braille invented a way to read and write for blind people. He was a teenager.

Theme Vocabulary

creative (adj.)
idea (n.)
solution (n.)
solve (v.)
wonder (v.)
youth (n.)

Word	Definition
youth	young people, especially teenagers
	a thought or plan about what to do
	having the ability to make new things or think of new ideas
	to find a way to end a problem; to find the answer
	a way of fixing a problem
	to be interested in knowing or learning something

PRACTICE 2 Work with a partner. Answer the questions about the conversation.

1. What current and past problems does the student talk about?
2. Why does the student think that young people are good at problem solving?
3. What is another problem that young people can solve?

Explore the Essential Question

Think How do you solve problems? Complete activities 1 and 2 below.

1. Check (✔) all the ways you solve problems.

☐ I brainstorm ideas with others.　　☐ I draw pictures of solutions.

☐ I ask an adult for help.　　　　　　☐ I research the problem.

☐ I work alone to solve the problem.　☐ I share my ideas with others.

2. Read the sentences. Place an (✗) on the line to show how strongly you agree or disagree.

	Strongly Disagree	Not Sure	Strongly Agree
1. Youth and adults can solve the same problems.	←		→
2. Youth are more creative than adults.	←		→
3. Young people ask more questions than adults.	←		→
4. Adults listen to young people's ideas and solutions.	←		→

Discuss With a partner, discuss your answers to activities 1 and 2 above.

Respond Circle the words related to solving problems. Add your own ideas. Then use some of the words to complete the sentence below. Share your ideas with a partner.

ask questions　**use social media**

read　make mistakes　listen

create solve problems

ask for help　do research　**talk**

use technology　make decisions

take notes　work together　**make lists**

To solve problems, young people should _____

and _____ .

Key Vocabulary

PRACTICE Look at the photos and read the sentences. Discuss the meaning of the words in **bold** with a partner. Then ask and answer the questions.

crowd (noun)
Many musicians attract a large **crowd**.
What other events have crowds?

figure out (verb phrase)
He is trying to **figure out** the math problem.
Are you good at figuring out math problems?

guess (verb)
A: **Guess** which cup has a ball under it.
B: The middle one?
Do you sometimes guess answers on tests?

huge (adjective)
An adult elephant is **huge**.
What other animals are huge?

riddle (noun)
A **riddle** is a type of puzzle to solve.
Try this riddle: What has four legs but cannot run?

weigh (verb)
You can use a scale to **weigh** many things.
How much does this person weigh?

Grammar: Count and Noncount Nouns

Count Nouns

Count nouns are nouns we can count with numbers. (*one* **eye**, *two* **eyes**)

- A singular count noun uses a singular verb. (*An eye* **opens** *and* **closes**.)
- Most plural count nouns end with -*s*. (**eyes**)
- A plural count noun uses a plural verb. (*Our eyes* **see**.)
- Some count nouns are spelled the same when singular and plural. (*one* **fish**, *two* **fish**)

Noncount Nouns

Noncount nouns are nouns we cannot count with numbers. (**air**, **fruit**)

- Use a singular verb with a noncount noun subject. (*Fruit* **tastes** *good*.)
- Noncount nouns can be organized into the following categories:

Liquids and Gases	Food
air, water, coffee, tea, milk, smoke	fruit, cheese, bread, rice
Feelings and Knowledge	**Nature**
intelligence, love, hate, information, news	land, lightning, rain, wind, fog

PRACTICE 1 Write *C* for each count noun and *NC* for each noncount noun.

1. _____ advice
2. _____ lake
3. _____ oil
4. _____ idea
5. _____ advisor

6. _____ sugar
7. _____ fish
8. _____ rain
9. _____ kilogram
10. _____ feet

PRACTICE 2 Circle the correct verb form that completes each sentence.

1. Food *give* / *gives* us energy.
2. The banana *taste* / *tastes* good.
3. His party *is* / *are* a surprise.
4. Air *take* / *takes* up space.

5. The juice *was* / *were* delicious.
6. Boats *sink* / *sinks* if water gets in.
7. The guests *look* / *looks* important.
8. The elephant *weigh* / *weighs* a lot.

ESSENTIAL QUESTION

What problems can young people solve?

First Thoughts

1. How tall is this giraffe? Imagine you need to figure out a giraffe's height. You only have a 10-foot (3-meter) measuring tape. Brainstorm ideas in a small group.

2. Write your best ideas here.

_____

_____

_____

_____

_____

3. Check (✔) your best idea above.

Discuss Read the sentences. Check (✔) the statements you agree with. Then discuss your answers with your group.

☐ Our best idea was our first idea.

☐ Our ideas were more creative because we worked together.

☐ Asking questions was part of our brainstorming process.

☐ Brainstorming was a quick way to find many ideas.

☐ We combined two or more ideas to find our solution.

☐ My group's ideas helped me think of new ideas, too.

Reading Skill: Analyze the Structure of a Drama

A **drama**, or play, is a story that is performed by actors on a stage. Most of the story is told through **dialogue**, or what the characters say. To understand a drama, analyze the different parts:

- **Cast of Characters:** This lists all the characters in the play.
- **Narrator:** The narrator tells what is happening in the play. Pay attention to the extra information the narrator gives about the story or characters.
- **Dialogue:** Dialogue is what the characters say to each other. Lines of dialogue are any words said by a character. Think about what the dialogue tells you about the characters.
- **Stage Directions:** These are instructions that tell the actors what to do. Visualize the actions as you read the dialogue.

Skill in Action

Read the excerpt from *Cao Chong Weighs an Elephant* and a reader's thoughts. Then complete the activities below.

Narrator 1 gives information about the characters' location and situation. I think this is an important event.

Each part of the dialogue begins with the character's name.

Narrator 1: Cao Cao led his son to the courtyard, where his father's advisors and hundreds of guests waited. Soon, the ambassador of the Wu Kingdom guided an enormous gray beast toward the crowd.
Cao Chong: (delighted) See how it takes one small nut at a time from the ambassador's hand and transfers it to its mouth?
Zhi: Yes, for such a huge animal, it is a dainty eater.
Narrator 2: Cao Chong ran up to the elephant and began to stroke its head …
Cao Chong: It has the most wonderful nose in the world …
Shun: This creature is amazing. How much must it weigh—5,000 jin?
Min: Its legs are like logs. And those feet are tree stumps. (tries to lift elephant's leg)

The stage directions say that Cao Chong is delighted, or happy. He's probably smiling.

The dialogue tells the reader what the characters say to each other. I can tell that Cao Chong likes the animal.

1. Read Narrator 2's line. Imagine Cao Chong's actions. Then read Cao Chong's line.
2. With three classmates, read the dialogue, each of you reading two characters' lines (and one reading the narrators' lines).
3. Circle Min's stage directions. Then act out the dialogue.

Read and answer the question: **What are the steps Cao Chong takes to weigh the elephant?**
As you read, underline any parts of the text you have questions about or find confusing.

Cao Chong Weighs an Elephant

retold by Pat Betteley

Cao Chong was born in A.D. 196 in China. He has been called China's most famous prodigy (an extremely talented young person). He died when he was 12 years old. This story is thought to be true. A historian included it in a book called *Records of the Three Kingdoms*.

Cast of Characters:

Narrator 1

Narrator 2

Narrator 3

Cao Chong, son of Cao Cao

Cao Cao, prime minister of Eastern Han, China, and father of Cao Chong

Zhi, Ambassador of the Wu Kingdom

Shun, Min, and Ying, advisors to the prime minister

∩ 2.1

1 **Narrator 1:** Two thousand years ago lived a boy named Cao Chong. He was the son of Cao Cao, the prime minister of Eastern Han. One sunny day, Cao Cao found his son sitting by the koi pond watching the graceful orange and white fish.

5 **Cao Chong:** Father, did you ever **wonder** how fish sleep in the water? And do they have ears? Can they hear us talking?

Cao Cao: (chuckling) I do not know, son. You have more questions than I have answers. But, for now, come with me. I want to show you my present from the emperor of the Wu Kingdom. It is a gigantic animal called an "elephant." It has never been seen in our kingdom before.

10

> **STOP & THINK**
> **Explain** Why does Cao Cao laugh when his son asks the questions about the fish?

Narrator 1:	Cao Cao led his son to the courtyard, where his father's advisors and hundreds of guests waited. Soon, the ambassador of the Wu Kingdom guided an enormous gray beast toward the **crowd**.
Cao Chong:	(delighted) See how it takes one small nut at a time from the ambassador's hand and transfers[1] it to its mouth?
Zhi:	Yes, for such a **huge** animal, it is a dainty[2] eater.
Narrator 2:	Cao Chong ran up to the elephant and began to stroke its head. The playful elephant gently wrapped its long trunk around the small boy.
Cao Chong:	It has the most wonderful nose in the world. It moves like an arm, but grips[3] like a hand!
Shun:	This creature is amazing. How much must it **weigh**—5,000 jin[4]?
Min:	Its legs are like logs. And those feet are tree stumps. (tries to lift elephant's leg) Ooomph! I give up. I would **guess** 6,000 jin, at least!
Ying:	If I measure how broad its chest is, and then how long its body is, I may be able to **figure out** its weight.

[1] **transfers** moves
[2] **dainty** graceful; tidy
[3] **grips** holds
[4] **jin** a unit of weight equal to 500 grams

Narrator 2:	The elephant seemed to roll its eyes and continued to eat nuts from Ambassador Zhi's hand.
Shun:	I think that this elephant weighs 7,000 jin.
Min:	I think that it weighs 8,000 jin!
Cao Cao:	Ambassador Zhi, do you know how much the elephant weighs?
Zhi:	I wish I could say, honorable Prime Minister. In my kingdom, elephants are too big and heavy for our scales. Surely, in such a wise kingdom as yours, the people will know a way to measure[5] it.
Cao Cao:	Let my present be our challenge, then. Learned advisors and guests, we must show Ambassador Zhi the power and intelligence of our kingdom. Who can find a way to determine the exact weight of this elephant?
Min:	I say we build a VERY large scale that will hold an elephant.
Ying:	That will not work. This animal is far too large to weigh on the scales we use to weigh food.
Shun:	He is right. To weigh an elephant, the arms of the scale would have to be huge, and the measuring pan would need to be the size of a small room.
Ying:	What if we slice the elephant into smaller pieces to fit a normal-sized scale?
Shun:	How cruel[6] to kill the elephant to learn its weight.
Cao Chong:	Father, I have an **idea**. (whispering into his father's ear)

STOP & THINK
Infer Why does the author write, "The elephant seemed to roll its eyes"?

---

[5] **measure** find the weight of
[6] **cruel** mean

Cao Cao:	Hmmm. That just may work!
Narrator 3:	So Cao Chong, his father, and all of the guests walked to the lake, where a wooden boat was tied up at the bank. The small boy guided the elephant onto the boat. The boat sank low into the water.
55 **Cao Chong:**	I will carve a line on the outside of the boat to mark the water line.
Narrator 3:	When Cao Chong led the elephant off the boat to land, the carved line on the boat rose higher above the water. The advisors were puzzled.
Shun:	What game are you playing, little one?
Cao Chong:	Now load[7] rocks into the boat. When the carved line on the boat sinks to the level of the water, we will weigh the rocks on a scale, a few at a time.
Narrator 1:	The crowd counted out loud as each load of rocks was weighed.
All:	Thirty-eight jin! Forty-two jin! Fifty-one jin!

60

---

[7] **load** put

Cao Chong: Now I will add up the weight of all the stones. Father, I have calculated the elephant's exact weight. It is 9,398 jin!

Narrator 1: The crowd clapped and cheered. Even the elephant seemed pleased.[8] It raised its trunk to blow water into the air.

Cao Cao: (hugging his son) Clever thinking, my son. You have **solved** the **riddle** of the elephant's weight and proven the intelligence of our kingdom to the whole world!

65

70

---

[8] **pleased** happy

Close Read

Work with a partner.

1. Determine the meanings of your underlined words and phrases.
2. Discuss the question:

   What are the steps Cao Chong takes to weigh the elephant?

Apply the Skill: Analyze the Structure of a Drama

Read the excerpt from the play. Then complete the activities below.

> **Ying:** What if we slice the elephant into smaller pieces to fit a normal-sized scale?
>
> **Shun:** How cruel to kill the elephant to learn its weight.
>
> **Cao Chong:** Father, I have an idea. (whispering into his father's ear)
>
> **Cao Cao:** Hmmm. That just may work!
>
> **Narrator 3:** So Cao Chong, his father, and all of the guests walked to the lake, where a wooden boat was tied up at the bank. The small boy guided the elephant onto the boat. The boat sank low into the water.

1. Put a check (✓) next to each character's name. Underline the first two lines of dialogue. Circle the stage directions.
2. What do the lines of dialogue tell you about Ying and Shun?
3. What do the stage directions tell you about Cao Chong?
4. Summarize the information that Narrator 3 shares.

   _____

   _____

Understand

Complete the sentences using the correct character's name from the play.

1. _____ wonders how much the huge elephant weighs.

2. _____ thinks someone from Han can figure out how to weigh the elephant.

3. _____ makes his present a challenge.

4. Cao Cao's advisors, _____ and _____, think of solutions for the problem. Their ideas do not help solve the riddle.

5. _____ figures out the riddle of how to weigh the elephant.

Read Again and Analyze

Read the text again and respond to the questions. Use evidence from the text to support your responses.

1. **Characterize** What are two words that describe Cao Chong?

2. **Identify** What ideas do the advisors suggest to solve the problem?

3. **Differentiate** Why don't Min's and Ying's solutions to the problem work? Why does Cao Chong's solution work?

4. **Distinguish** Which character makes the best guess of how many jin the elephant weighs? What is his guess?

Share Your Perspective

Discuss the questions in a small group.

1. Shun asks Cao Chong, "What game are you playing, little one?" What does Shun's word choice tell you about what he thinks about Cao Chong?

2. Cao Chong asks many questions. How can asking questions help solve problems?

3. When can questions help you solve a problem? Give an example.

Discussion Frames

Shun does/doesn't think Cao Chong …

Asking questions helps solve problems because …

Questions can help me solve a problem when I …

Reflect

How does *Cao Chong Weighs an Elephant* help you understand what problems young people can solve? With a partner, use some of the words to write sentences about the text.

Nouns	Verbs	Adjectives
crowd	figure out	creative
idea	guess	huge
riddle	solve	
solution	weigh	
youth	wonder	

_____

_____

_____

Fixing Fashion

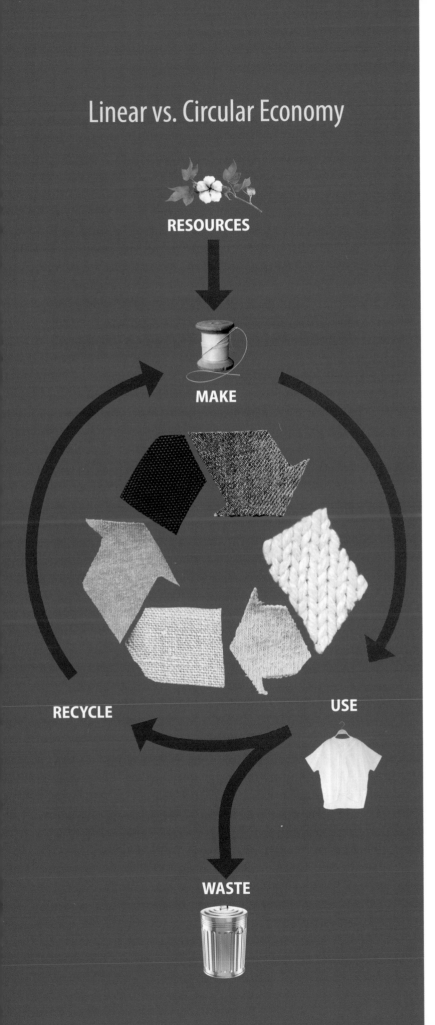

Linear vs. Circular Economy

RESOURCES

MAKE

RECYCLE

USE

WASTE

Examine the Graphic

Use details from the image and the text to respond to the questions. Discuss your responses with a partner.

1. What does the graphic make you think about?

2. What is something you find surprising?

3. What is a *circular economy*?

4. What does the graphic say happens to old clothes?

Make Connections

Use details from the image and the text to discuss your responses with a partner.

1. How is the photo related to the linear part of the graphic?

2. What do you think this photo is trying to say about clothing or fashion? Do you agree or disagree with this idea?

Reflect

Use ideas from the graphic and your responses to answer the question: What is another global problem that a circular economy can help to solve? Explain how it could help to solve the problem.

◀ **A *linear* economy uses natural resources to make clothing or other products and then throws them away. A *circular* economy reuses the products rather than throwing them away.**

Key Vocabulary

PRACTICE Look at the photos and read the sentences. Discuss the meaning of the words in **bold** with a partner. Then ask and answer the questions.

able (adjective)
She is **able** to snowboard well.
What are you able to do well?

global (adjective)
The United Nations is a **global** organization.
What is another global organization you know about?

improve (verb)
The boy **improved** his test score. His last test score was 70%.
How can students improve their grades?

information (noun)
I found **information** about lions on this website.
Where do you get information when you write a report?

issue (noun)
Pollution is an **issue** in many cities.
What is an environmental issue in your area?

try (verb)
He's going to **try** to ride a bike.
When did you last try something new?

Vocabulary: Understand Problem/Solution Signal Words

Signal words are words that can help you understand the organization of a text. In a problem/solution text, identifying words that indicate a problem or solution can help you better understand the text. Some common problem/solution signal words include:

	Problem	Solution
Nouns	issue, problem, reason	idea, solution
Verbs	cause	solve, improve, try
Conjunctions	because, but, so	so

To understand problem/solution relationships in a text, think about these ideas:

1. Which signal words indicate a problem? Which signal words indicate a solution?

2. What information do these signal words add?

3. How can you summarize the problem and solution in your own words?

Example:

Three high school students in Singapore had an idea to improve supercapacitors. These devices store energy. Most supercapacitors are stiff, so there is a limit to where they can be used. Their inventive solution was a supercapacitor that can be painted onto anything, even fabric and paper.

Idea and *improve* are signal words for a solution. This sentence indicates that the students solved a problem with supercapacitors.

So is a signal word for a problem in this sentence. This sentence talks about a problem with supercapacitors.

Here's the word *solution* and more specifics about the supercapacitor that the students designed.

PRACTICE Read the second paragraph of "Youthquake!" Complete the chart with the signal word. Then write the problem and three solutions that were tried.

	Problem	Solutions
Signal Words		
Summary		

ESSENTIAL QUESTION

What problems can young people solve?

First Thoughts

1. With a partner, write three sentences to explain what is happening in the photo.

2. What problem are the people in the photo working on? Write words and phrases that describe the problem and solution.

Problem: _____

Solution: _____

3. Write a title for the photo. _____

Discuss Look at the photos. What ideas do you have for solving these problems? Write your ideas. Then discuss your answers with a partner.

Reading Strategy: Ask Questions

Good readers **ask questions** as they read. This helps them better understand what they are reading. Follow these steps to ask questions as you read:

1. As you read, pause regularly to ask questions.

2. What are you wondering about? Is there something you don't understand? Ask *wh-* (*who, what, when, where, why*) and *how* questions about the text.

3. Try to find answers to your questions in the text.

Strategy in Action

Read the paragraph and a reader's questions. Then complete the activities below.

An "innovation" is a new idea or way of doing something. For example, audio sunglasses (sunglasses that play music!) are an innovation. They were introduced in 2019. A "social innovation" helps people or the environment. For example, Thato Kgatlhanye is a young social innovator from South Africa. She makes backpacks with lights for schoolchildren. The sun charges the light's battery during the day. At night, kids without electricity can use the lights to do their homework.

Audio sunglasses? Cool! When were they invented?

What does *innovation* mean?

I wonder what *social innovation* means.

Why are the backpacks with lights an example of a social innovation?

1. Circle the text that explains what *innovation* and *social innovation* mean.

2. Underline the text that answers the reader's other questions: "When were audio sunglasses invented?" "Why are the backpacks with lights an example of a social innovation?"

3. What questions do you have about the text?

_____

_____

_____

_____

Read and answer the question: **What problems are discussed in the text?**
As you read, underline any parts of the text you have questions about or
find confusing.

Youthquake!

by **Judith Lipsett**

⌒ 2.2

1 In 2017, *youthquake* was Oxford Dictionary's word of the year.
As everyone knows, an earthquake shakes things up. A *youthquake*
is defined as important change started by young people. That
suggests that **youth** can also shake things up—but in a positive
5 way! All around the world, young people are finding **creative
solutions** to important **global** problems.

Take Richard Turere, for example. Richard is a young Maasai
herder in Kenya, Africa. He doesn't have an **issue** with lions in
general. But he did have an issue with the lions killing his family's
10 cows at night. So Richard **tried** different **ideas** to protect their
cows. First, he used a scarecrow.[1] That didn't **solve** the problem.
Then he built a dark shed so that the lions couldn't see the cows.
That didn't help either. One night, Richard patrolled[2] outside with
a flashlight. The light made the lions stay away. They were afraid of
15 the moving light. This gave him the idea for Lion Lights.

Richard learned about electronics by taking things apart,
including his mother's new radio. Using a car battery and a solar
panel, he put LED lights on poles. He then made the lights flash
on and off. It looked like a person with a flashlight, so the lions
20 stopped attacking the cows. Thanks to Lion Lights, the lions were
also in less danger of being killed by farmers. Because of Richard's
creative problem-solving, Lion Lights can now be found on more
than 750 Maasai homesteads.

> **STOP & THINK**
> **Differentiate**
> Which idea solved
> Richard's problem?

---

[1] **scarecrow** a human-shaped object used to scare off animals
[2] **patrolled** checked for trouble

Richard Turere, 13, attaches his Lion Lights to protect cows near his home on the outskirts of Nairobi National Park, Kenya.

There are over 1.2 billion young people between the ages of 15 and 24. That number is expected to grow. Youth like Richard have shown that they want to make a difference. They want to help their communities solve global problems. Recognizing this, the United Nations created a free messaging app called U-Report. On U-Report, young people in 68 countries can share their opinions about issues that impact their lives. Topics they discuss include how to **improve** education, how to raise awareness[3] about climate change, or how to transition to a green economy.

STOP & THINK
Cite What evidence in the text supports the fact that U-Report is a global program?

Using U-Report, youth can also access "bots" that help them learn about specific issues. The U-Report COVID-19 chatbot shared **information** about the virus. More than six million young people in 52 countries interacted with the chatbot. The program also gives its users a tool to organize themselves in emergencies. For example, when a flood[4] hit Côte D'Ivoire in 2018, young U-Reporters there were immediately **able** to help with clean up.

More than 4,600 miles from Richard's home, three young women in Singapore also wanted to use technology to solve problems. High school students Marion Pang Wan Rion, Joy Ang Jing Zhi, and Sonia Arumuganainar had an idea to improve supercapacitors. These are devices that store[5] energy. They are found in cars, laptop computers, and smart devices such as watches and phones. Supercapacitors are better for the environment than regular batteries. They last longer and do not contain toxic substances. However, most supercapacitors are stiff,[6] so there is a limit to where they can be used. The three young women **wondered** if the devices could be flexible. Their creative solution was a supercapacitor that can be painted onto surfaces[7] like fabric or paper, or even added to car paint! The students' work is part of the global push towards more sustainable energy.

STOP & THINK
Explain How did the students improve supercapacitors?

---

[3] **raise awareness** build knowledge
[4] **flood** high water
[5] **store** collect to use later
[6] **stiff** difficult to bend
[7] **surfaces** sides or top layer

Richard, U-Reporters, and the students from Singapore all
aim to improve their communities and the world. They are all part
of the "youthquake." And they share the qualities that a fellow
Kenyan saw in Richard Turere. She said, "He's not afraid of being
unable to do something, and I think this is why he is such a good
innovator—because he's not worried that it might not work, he's
going to try and do it anyway."

U-Reporters working in Thailand

Close Read

Work with a partner.

1. Determine the meanings of your underlined words and phrases.
2. Discuss the question:

What problems are discussed in the text?

Apply the Strategy: Ask Questions

Write three questions you asked or wondered as you read. Then write the answers you found in the text.

Question	Answer

Understand

Circle the problems. Underline the solutions. Then compare your answers with a partner.

1. Lions ate the family's cows, so Richard Turere created Lion Lights.

2. U-Report sent young people in Côte D'Ivoire ideas and information about how to help their communities after a flood in 2018.

3. Supercapacitors were stiff. Three high school students from Singapore figured out how to improve them by making them flexible.

Read Again and Analyze

Read the text again and respond to the questions. Use evidence from the text to support your responses.

1. **Deduce** How is Richard Turere creative?
2. **Evaluate** Which innovation in the text do you think helps the most people?
3. **Compare** How are all the innovations in the text similar?
4. **Give Examples** When do young people use U-Report?
5. **Apply** What topics or information in your city would be useful for U-reporters to discuss or learn about?

Share Your Perspective

Discuss the questions in a small group.

1. What global problem would you like to solve?
2. What information would you need to solve the problem?
3. What could other people do to help you solve the problem?

Discussion Frames

The global problem I would like to solve is …

I would need information about …

People could help me …

Reflect

How does "Youthquake!" help you understand what problems young people can solve? With a partner, use some of the words to write sentences about the text.

Nouns	Verbs	Adjectives
idea information issue solution youth	improve solve try wonder	able creative global

_____

_____

_____

Teen Invents Sensor to Help Patients with Dementia

Kenneth Shinozuka
with his grandfather

First Thoughts

Sensors detect things such as heat, light, or movement and trigger a reaction. Look at each picture. What does each item detect? What reaction happens?

Example: *A smoke alarm detects smoke. It triggers an alarm.*

| **smoke alarm** | **scale** | **touchscreen** |

Viewing Skill: Identify Details

We can learn more about a topic by identifying details in a video. When you watch a video, listen for the topic. Then listen for details about the topic.

Apply the Skill

▶ **2.1** Watch the video. Check (✔) the details you hear about Shinozuka's product.

☐ The sensor triggers an alarm.

☐ The sensor wakes up the patient.

☐ The tracking goes to a smartphone.

☐ The sensor is attached to the wrist.

Understand and Analyze

▶ **2.1** Watch the video again. Answer the questions. Support your responses with evidence from the video.

1. **Explain** Why is there a pressure sensor?
2. **Conclude** Why does the sensor trigger an alarm?
3. **Correlate** What idea did Shinozuka have after observing his grandfather getting out of bed?
4. **Infer** What are some ways the device might help Shinozuka's aunt?

Share Your Perspective

Discuss the questions in a small group.

1. What is a family or community problem you would like to solve?
2. How could you solve the problem?

Discussion Frames

A problem I would like to solve is …

I could solve it by …

First, I would …

Reflect on the Essential Question

Think about the characters and young people in this unit. What are the problems they solved? Write your ideas in the idea web.

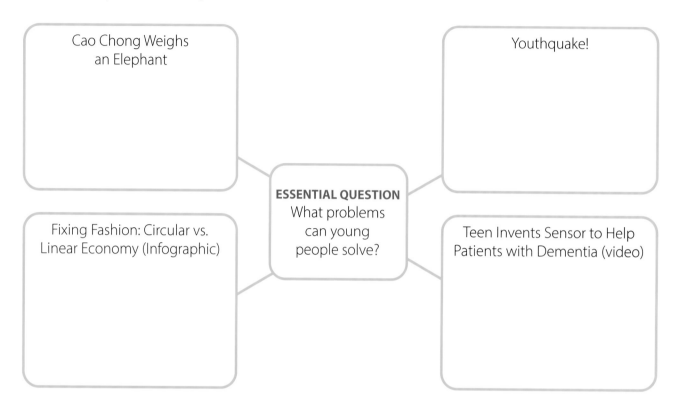

Cao Chong Weighs an Elephant

Youthquake!

Fixing Fashion: Circular vs. Linear Economy (Infographic)

ESSENTIAL QUESTION
What problems can young people solve?

Teen Invents Sensor to Help Patients with Dementia (video)

Discuss the Essential Question

Look at your ideas about the Essential Question earlier in the unit and your notes in the idea web above. How have your ideas about the Essential Question changed? What changed your ideas? Discuss your answers in a group.

Respond to the Essential Question

Write your response to the Essential Question.

Theme Vocabulary

creative (adj.)
idea (n.)
solution (n.)
solve (v.)
wonder (v.)
youth (n.)

Response Rubric
A good response will
✓ state your opinion
✓ provide support from the texts, the discussion, and your life
✓ use theme vocabulary

Option 1: Present an Elevator Pitch

An **elevator pitch** is a short presentation of a business idea. It is short enough that you could explain your idea during an elevator ride. Look at the example elevator pitch using the problem and solution in *Cao Chong Weighs an Elephant*. Then create your own elevator pitch.

1. Think of a problem. You can create an elevator pitch for any problem from the unit, or for another global problem such as hunger, poverty, or pollution.
2. Complete a chart like the following.
3. Practice giving your elevator pitch to a partner.

Example:

Introduction	I'd like to tell you about a problem I want to solve.
What is the problem?	The problem is that it is difficult to weigh an elephant because it is too large to weigh on scales.
What is the outcome?	When we solve this problem, people will know how much the elephant weighs.
What is the solution?	We can solve this problem by putting the elephant on a boat and marking the water level. Then we will lead the elephant off the boat and fill the boat with rocks until it reaches the water level we marked. After that, we will weigh the rocks. That weight is the elephant's weight.
Why is this the best solution?	This is the best solution because it doesn't hurt the elephant.

Option 2: Create an Advertisement

In the article "Youthquake!", young people solved various problems. Advertising their solutions can help other people in the world benefit from these ideas.

1. Decide which solution you will create an advertisement for (Lion Lights, U-Report, flexible supercapacitors, or find another idea).
2. Decide who the advertisement is for and consider what they need to know about the solution.
3. Include the benefits. How will the product help the people the ad is for?
4. Create your advertisement on a piece of paper or in a drawing program. Include an image of the product or the idea.

Assignment: Write an Expository Text

An **expository text** is one that explains or gives information about a topic. In this assignment, you will write a short paragraph about a problem that a young person or young people solved. Your paragraph should include:

- a title that gives a clue about the problem or solution
- an introduction that describes the problem
- sentences that describe the solution with at least three details
- problem/solution signal words
- a picture or drawing of the person or solution
- a concluding sentence that states the impact or benefit of the solution

Explore the Model

Read the model. Look at the details about the invention that the writer includes. Underline all the sentences with details about the invention.

Language for Writing

Read the model again.

1. Identify the signal words that describe the problem and solution.

Problem Signal Words	Solution Signal Words

2. Find examples of count and noncount nouns in the text. Write two examples in each column.

Singular Count Nouns	Plural Count Nouns	Noncount Nouns

3. The writer sometimes uses a pronoun instead of a noun that has already been introduced. Complete the sentences with the correct pronouns.

Satellites are big and expensive. Only big, rich countries can buy them because _____ cost millions of dollars.

Space Kidz India solved this problem. _____ are high school and college students in India.

The Space Kidz team celebrates the successful launch of the satellite KalamSat from NASA's Wallops Island facility in Chennai, India.

The photo shows the solution that is described in the paragraph.

Space Kidz Creates a Lighter Satellite

The introduction describes the problem.

The writer uses signal words like "because" to discuss the problem and solution.

This sentence includes the first detail about the solution.

The concluding sentence states the impact or benefit of the solution.

Satellites are big and expensive. Only big, rich countries can buy them because they cost millions of dollars. Space Kidz India solved this problem. They are high school and college students in India. They built the world's lightest satellite. The team did a lot of research. Then it took six days to build the satellite. The satellite weighs 64 grams. The team's idea makes satellites small. It also makes satellite technology cheap. Their solution means many people, including students, can launch a satellite.

Plan Your Writing

Complete the outline.

- Research a problem that a young person solved.
- Write information about the problem in the outline.
- Write details about the solution and its impact.
- Add a title that gives a clue about the problem or solution.

Outline

Title	
Problem	What is the problem?
Solution	What is the solution?
	What three important details about the solution will you include?
	What is the impact or benefit of the solution?

Write and Revise

Write Use your outline to write a first draft.

- Use signal words to write about the problem and solution.
- Use the correct verb form with count and noncount nouns.

Revise Exchange expository texts with a partner. Using the checklist, review your partner's work and give feedback. Use feedback from your partner to revise your draft.

Feedback Frames

I like how you explain …

This detail shows …

I think you should add …

☐	Does the introduction describe the problem?
☐	Does the writer include at least three details about the solution?
☐	Does the writer include a picture or drawing of the person or the solution?
☐	Does the concluding sentence state the impact or benefit of the solution?

Proofread Check the grammar, spelling, punctuation, and capitalization in your text. Make edits to correct any errors.

TIP

Check the spelling in your text. Use your computer spelling program or a dictionary to help you. Check that you've used the correct verb form with count and noncount nouns.

Publish

Share your expository text. Read two of your classmates' texts.

Present Your Expository Text

You will share your paragraph with a group. When you present the information, pause and make eye contact with the audience a few times during the presentation.

Prepare to share your expository text and picture or drawing:

- Practice presenting your text to a partner. Try not to read during your presentation.
- Remember to look up a few times during your presentation.

Share your expository text in a small group.

- Listen to each presenter. Ask questions after the presentation.
- Give feedback. You can say, "I like the detail about …" or "I can tell that this solution is …"

Grey crowned cranes stand together at a rehabilitation facility in Rwanda.

Finding Solutions for the Grey Crowned Crane 🎧 2.3

EXPLORER IN ACTION

Olivier Nsengimana
is a veterinarian and crane conservationist. He founded the Rwanda Wildlife Conservation Association.

As a child, Olivier Nsengimana and his friends loved to watch grey crowned cranes dance in the green grasses near their village in Rwanda. In the past, there were many of these cranes. When Olivier started his work, however, there were fewer than 500 in Rwanda. Now a young veterinarian, Nsengimana is working with the government and people around the country to help the cranes in two ways. First, he is working to teach others to protect the cranes and their wetland habitats. Second, he is helping to return the cranes to the wild. People used to catch the beautiful birds and keep them as pets. Nsengimana locates these pets and then returns them to the wild. So far, 319 cranes from homes and hotels have been brought to a rehabilitation facility. At the facility, they are taught how to survive in the wild. Nsengimana has helped return 166 of these cranes to nature. Nsengimana's creative solutions mean the number of grey crowned cranes is increasing in Rwanda for the first time in many years.

▶ **2.2** Complete the sentences. Then watch the video to learn more.

1. The problem Nsengimana is working on is _____ .

2. His solution focuses on _____ and _____ .

How Will You Take Action?

Choose one or more of these actions to do.

Personal

Map solutions.

1. In the middle of a piece of paper, name a problem you have.
2. Use words or pictures to describe the problem.
3. For each phrase or picture describing the problem, write or draw a solution.
4. Discuss your problem and possible solutions with a partner.

School

Solve personal problems together.

1. Set up an anonymous advice box where students can ask for help with a personal problem, such as what to do about a bad grade or a time-management issue.
2. Read each problem. Assign a small group to brainstorm solutions.
3. Share the solutions with the entire class.

Local

Research social innovation.

1. Find a young person or group in your community that used social innovation to solve a problem.
2. Ask interview questions about the solution and the problem it solves.
3. Illustrate a poster with the details you collect. Share your poster with your class.

Global

Help solve global problems.

1. Join a group such as U-Report or Global Youth Mobilization.
2. Participate in online or in-person events for an issue that interests you.
3. Share what you learn with other youth and adults.

Reflect

Reflect on your Take Action project(s). Then complete the sentences.

1. My project(s) was/were successful because

   _____.

2. One thing I wish I had done differently is

   _____.

3. Because of what I learned in this unit, one thing I will do is

   _____.

3 Perspective

"If you look the right way, you can see that the whole world is a garden."

—FRANCES HODGSON BURNETT, BRITISH-AMERICAN NOVELIST

What does this quote mean to you?

Look at the photo and caption. Discuss the questions.

1. How is this photo unusual?

2. How does this close-up view change the way you think about dandelions?

◀ **Close-up of dandelion seeds**

ESSENTIAL QUESTION

Why do people see the same things differently?

Theme Vocabulary

Use these words to express your ideas throughout the unit.

PRACTICE 1 Read the conversation. Think about the meaning of each word in **bold**. Then write each word next to its definition in the chart below.

> When have you had a **perspective** different from someone else's?

> My parents said piano lessons would be good for me. I **disagreed**. My parents think music and art are important. My mother has lots of **experience** playing the piano. She says it helps with stress. My father wanted me to play for another **reason**. He said it would make me smarter. I saw the situation **differently**. I had so much homework. I didn't want more work. We made the **decision** to try one lesson a week. I actually really like it!

Theme Vocabulary

decision (n.)
differently (adv.)
disagree (v.)
experience (n.)
perspective (n.)
reason (n.)

Word	Definition
decision	a choice you make after thinking about it
	something that happens to you that affects how you feel or act
	in a way that is not the same
	a statement that explains why someone acts or thinks a certain way
	a way of thinking about something
	to not have the same opinion or idea

PRACTICE 2 Work with a partner. Answer the questions about the conversation.

1. Who has experience playing the piano?
2. What reason did the student give for not wanting to play the piano?
3. What reasons did the mother and father give for wanting the student to learn piano?

Explore the Essential Question

Think When have you had a perspective different from a friend's or family member's?

1. What was the situation? What was your perspective? What was the other person's perspective? Did you agree on anything? Why were your perspectives different? Take notes in the chart.

Situation	
My perspective	
Other's perspective	
Why were your perspectives different?	
Did you understand each other's perspective?	

2. Think about your answers. Check (✔) the ideas that were true for you.

- ☐ Our experiences were different.
- ☐ Our reasons were different.
- ☐ We understood each other's reasons.
- ☐ We agreed in the end.
- ☐ We disagreed in the end.
- ☐ I felt good about the decision/discussion.

Discuss With a partner, discuss activities 1 and 2 above. Give examples.

Respond Circle the words related to the idea of perspective. Add your own ideas. Then use some of the words to complete the sentence below. Share your ideas with a partner.

fear actions **feelings**

listening changing life

facts **perspective** personal

understanding truth

emotions agreeing

priorities **thoughts**

People have different perspectives because

Key Vocabulary

PRACTICE Look at the photos and read the sentences. Discuss the meaning of the words in **bold** with a partner. Then ask and answer the questions.

alive (adjective)
This plant is **alive**.
What do plants need to stay alive?

borrow (verb)
When I don't have a pencil, I **borrow** one from a friend.
What have you borrowed from a friend?

dangerous (adjective)
Hippos are **dangerous**. They kill 500 people a year!
What other animals are dangerous?

dead (adjective)
These plants are **dead**.
How do you know if a plant is dead?

net (noun)
The fish are caught in a **net**.
What else can you catch with a net?

save (verb)
Lifeguards can **save** people.
What is another job where people save lives?

Grammar: Prepositions of Place and Direction

Prepositions of place are words that give information about where someone or something is located. **Prepositions of direction** are words that give information about which way someone or something is moving or facing. Prepositions are followed by a noun or a noun phrase (examples: *on the boat, into the water*).

Prepositions of Place	Prepositions of Direction	
 The boy is **in** the boat.	 The whale is diving **into** the water.	 The boat is moving **toward** the whale.
 The man is standing **on** the beach.	 The whale is jumping **out of** the water.	 The boat is moving **away from** the whale.

PRACTICE 1 Complete each sentence with the correct **bold** preposition from the chart above.

1. The whale swam _____*toward*_____ the small fish and ate them.

2. A few fish swam _____ the whale and were safe.

3. The boy was hot, so he jumped _____ the water.

4. The boy got _____ the water when his dad called him for dinner.

5. They ate dinner _____ the beach.

PRACTICE 2 Use the words to write a sentence. Use a correct form of the verb, and add a preposition of place or direction.

1. turtle / swam / beach

_____

2. children / jump / water

_____

3. turtle / swim / boat

_____

ESSENTIAL QUESTION

Why do people see the same things differently?

First Thoughts

1. What do you see in the photo? Tell a partner.

2. Is it a good idea for humans to be this close to a whale? Give one reason why it's a good idea and one reason why it's not a good idea.

_____

_____

3. Write a title for the photo.

_____

Discuss Read the statements. Rank them from 1 (least important) to 5 (most important). Discuss your answers with a group.

_____ It is important to protect animals in danger.

_____ It is important to do what you think is right.

_____ It is important to obey adults.

_____ It is important to be safe.

_____ It is important to take action even when you are scared.

Reading Strategy: Describe a Story's Plot

The **plot** is the series of events in a story. Every story has a problem, or **conflict**. Most stories also have these parts:

1. **Exposition:** The characters and setting are introduced.
2. **Rising Action:** The conflict is introduced. A series of events happen.
3. **Climax:** The most exciting part of the story happens.
4. **Falling Action:** The conflict is being solved or ends.
5. **Resolution:** The plot ends. The conflict is solved.

Strategy in Action

Review the plot diagram for *Cao Chong Weighs an Elephant* from Unit 2. With a partner, think of another story or movie you both know. Complete a plot diagram for that story or movie on a separate piece of paper. Share your completed diagram with another group.

Plot of *Cao Chong Weighs an Elephant*

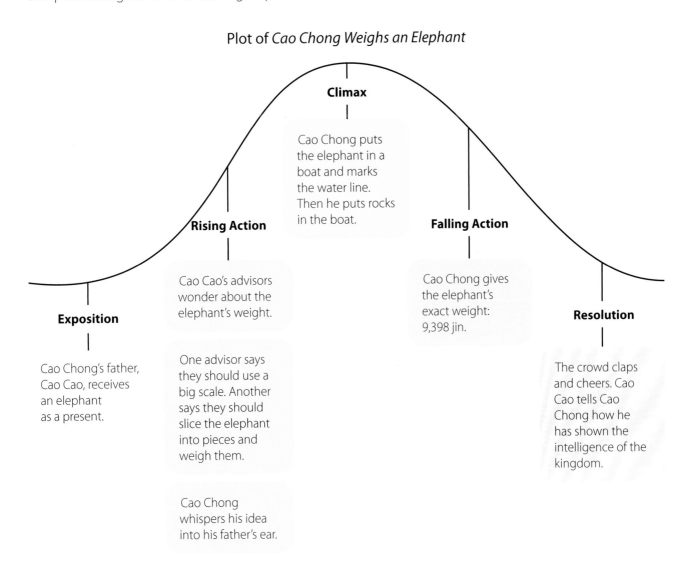

Climax

Cao Chong puts the elephant in a boat and marks the water line. Then he puts rocks in the boat.

Rising Action

Cao Cao's advisors wonder about the elephant's weight.

One advisor says they should use a big scale. Another says they should slice the elephant into pieces and weigh them.

Cao Chong whispers his idea into his father's ear.

Falling Action

Cao Chong gives the elephant's exact weight: 9,398 jin.

Exposition

Cao Chong's father, Cao Cao, receives an elephant as a present.

Resolution

The crowd claps and cheers. Cao Cao tells Cao Chong how he has shown the intelligence of the kingdom.

Read and answer the question: **What does the boy do?** As you read, underline any parts of the text you have questions about or find confusing.

The Boy and the Whale

*by **Mordicai Gerstein***

🎧 **3.1**

1   Every day, I loved to watch the sun rise out of the sea. One morning I saw something in the water. Something big. "That's a whale out there," said Papa. "It looks **dead**." We jumped into our panga[1] for a closer look. "Oh no!" yelled Papa. He cursed[2] the
5   whale with words I'd never heard him say. "It's tangled in our **net**! Our *only* net! I hope we can **save** it!" "Save the whale, Papa?" "No, my son, save our net! The whale is dead."

We dived into the water. I had never been so close to an animal so huge. Wrapped by the net in a hopeless tangle, the whale must
10   have died unable to move. I had been tangled in a net once, too. I almost drowned. Papa saved me. The whale's closed eye was as big as my head. And then it blinked! And I had to … BREATHE!

---
[1] **panga** small boat
[2] **cursed** said bad words about

> **STOP & THINK**
> **Contrast** What does the father mean when he says, "I hope we can save it!"? What does the boy think the word *it* means?

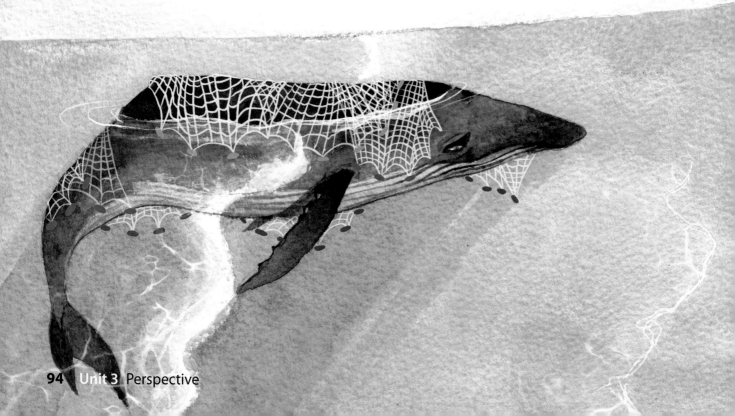

So did the whale. "Papa," I gasped. "The whale's **alive**!" "Just barely[3]," said Papa. "But our net is *ruined*! We have no money for a new one!" He turned the boat toward the shore. "Maybe," he said, "we can try to fix my uncle's old net and **borrow** it." "But … what about the whale?" I said. "The whale?" said Papa. "Maybe we should free it," I said. "Do you know," said Papa, "how difficult and **dangerous** that would be?" "But it might live …" "It destroyed our net!" said Papa. "How will we live?"

"I'm going to see my uncle. Forget the whale, and don't do anything foolish." "Yes, Papa," I said. I looked back out at the whale. I remembered being caught in the net, feeling helpless, and the awful fear. What does the whale feel? It's so big. I couldn't free it myself. If I tried, Papa would be very angry. I stood there for a long while. Then I jumped into the panga and headed for the whale. I had to try.

___
[3] **Just barely** Only a little

STOP & THINK
Explain Why is the net important to the father?

I took my fishing knife, hoped the whale wouldn't slap me with its tail, and dived in. I began to cut away the tough plastic netting. There was so much of it. Maybe Papa was right. I dived and cut and dived again – If only I didn't have to … BREATHE! I was getting tired. How much longer, I wondered, could I do this? *Whale*, I thought, *Do you have a name? Mine is Abelardo. I'm so very sorry about the net, Whale, but fishing is how we live. Do you know I'm trying my best to save you? But I don't know if I can …* When I looked again into the whale's eye, all I saw was my own reflection. *Don't die, Whale! I'm doing my best!*

But then … the net began to drift loose. Out of the water, I worked at pulling the net away from the whale. It filled the boat, but there was still more. Then I saw the whale move a flipper! And all at once … the whale was FREE! It sped away from the boat, and I cheered "Good-bye, Whale! Good-bye!" It dived … and disappeared. It BURST[4] out of the water, leaped into the sky, spun

[4] **burst** quickly moved

> **STOP & THINK**
> **Interpret** What information do the words in *italics* provide?

around, crashed back into the sea … and out again. The whale
45 slapped its tail, leaped again and again, forward and backward,
higher and higher! On and on! *Are you dancing to thank me, Whale?*
Or just for the joy of being free?

I watched the whale until it vanished[5] into the sea. Papa was
watching too, waiting on the beach. I went to face him. "You
50 actually did it?" he said. "Yes, Papa." "You disobeyed[6] me?" "Yes,
Papa," I said. "It was incredibly foolish!" said Papa. "And it was
very brave. Now come, my uncle's net needs fixing." "Yes, Papa!"
I said.

---

[5] **vanished** disappeared
[6] **disobeyed** didn't listen to

STOP & THINK
Word Choice Why do
you think the author
includes words like
BURST, leaped, and
higher and higher to
describe the whale after
it is free?

**About the Author:
Mordicai Gerstein
(1935–2019)**

Mordicai Gerstein wrote
many children's books,
including *The Man Who
Walked Between the
Towers,* for which he
won a Caldecott Medal.

The Boy and the Whale   **97**

Close Read

Work with a partner.

1. Determine the meanings of your underlined words and phrases.

2. Discuss the question:

What does the boy do?

Understand

PRACTICE 1   Who said or thought each statement from the text? Write *F* for father and *A* for Abelardo.

_____ **1.** "The whale is dead."

_____ **2.** "Maybe we should free it."

_____ **3.** "How will we live?"

_____ **4.** *Do you know I'm trying my best to save you?*

_____ **5.** "Good-bye, Whale! Good-bye!"

_____ **6.** "It was incredibly foolish! ... And it was very brave."

PRACTICE 2   Choose the best answer to complete the questions.

1. Abelardo's father *believed / didn't believe* saving the whale was a good idea.

2. Abelardo *saved / didn't save* the whale.

3. Abelardo *did / didn't do* what his father wanted.

4. Abelardo's father was *proud of / disappointed in* Abelardo at the end of the story.

5. Abelardo was *happy / upset* at the end of the story.

Apply the Strategy: Describe a Story's Plot

Match the details from the story to the correct story part.

_____ **1.** Exposition   **a.** His father says Abelardo was brave.

_____ **2.** Rising Action (1)   **b.** Abelardo tries to save the whale.

_____ **3.** Rising Action (2)   **c.** Abelardo and his father find a whale tangled in their net.

_____ **4.** Climax   **d.** Abelardo frees the whale from the net.

_____ **5.** Falling Action   **e.** Abelardo returns to the beach.

_____ **6.** Resolution   **f.** His father is upset because they need the net to live.

Read Again and Analyze

Read the text again and respond to the questions. Use evidence from the text to support your responses.

1. **Recognize** What evidence in the text supports the idea that the whale is dangerous?

2. **Compare** How is Abelardo's experience similar to the whale's experience?

3. **Conclude** Why isn't the father angry with Abelardo at the end of the story?

4. **Deduce** Why do you think the author included this line in the story? "When I looked again into the whale's eye, all I saw was my own reflection."

5. **Characterize** Is it easy for Abelardo to disobey his father? How do you know?

Share Your Perspective

Discuss the questions in a small group.

1. How do you think Abelardo would feel if he hadn't tried to save the whale? Why?

2. Was Abelardo foolish or brave to save the whale? Why?

3. Would you have tried to save the whale? Why or why not?

Discussion Frames

Abelardo would feel …

Abelardo was foolish/ brave. I think this because …

I would/wouldn't have tried to save the whale because …

Reflect

How does *The Boy and the Whale* help you understand why people see the same things differently? With a partner, use some of the words to write sentences about the story.

Nouns	Verbs	Adjectives/Adverbs
decision experience net perspective reason	borrow disagree save	alive dangerous dead differently

_____

_____

_____

UNCOVER THE STORY

Examine the Art

1. Look at the painting. Describe what you see.

2. Is your perspective different from your classmates'?

3. Write 3–5 questions about the painting. Discuss your questions with a small group.

Find Out ▶ 3.1

Watch the video about the artist and the painting.

1. Were your questions answered? Which ones?

2. What is the painting of? Do you see it in the painting?

3. What were the steps in making the painting? Who was involved?

Reflect

Aidan Meller says Ai-Da's work is creative because it's new, surprising, and has value. Do you agree? Why or why not?

Share Your Story

Share artwork with your class.

1. With a partner, choose an object for both of you to draw or paint.

2. Draw, paint, or create other artwork of the object. Do not show your partner your work.

3. When you are both finished, share your artwork with each other. How is the object similar or different?

4. Display your artwork for the class. Discuss how your perspectives of the object were the same or different.

ABOUT THE ARTIST

Ai-Da is known for portrait sketches and abstract paintings. Ai-Da began drawing and painting in 2019. Over one million dollars worth of Ai-Da's artwork has already been sold.

Key Vocabulary

PRACTICE Look at the photos and read the sentences. Discuss the meaning of the words in **bold** with a partner. Then ask and answer the questions.

concert (noun)
The musicians are giving a **concert**.
What kind of concert have you seen?

entertainment (noun)
Many people enjoy **entertainment**, like going to a play, movie, or opera.
What kind of entertainment do you like?

experiment (noun)
The student is doing a science **experiment**.
What kind of science experiments have you done?

notice (verb)
Do you **notice** anything strange about this photograph? Look closely.
How long did it take you to notice the insect in the photograph?

recognize (verb)
Smartphones now **recognize** people's faces.
Would you recognize your first teacher if you saw her or him?

respect (noun)
One way to show **respect** is to listen when someone talks.
What is another way to show respect?

Vocabulary: Prefixes That Mean *Not*

Prefixes can be added to the beginning of many words. A prefix changes the meaning of a word. The prefixes *dis-, im-, in-,* and *un-* can all mean *not*. You can use the meaning of a prefix to help you understand the meaning of a word.

dislike	**im**polite	**in**correct	**un**true
not like	not polite	not correct	not true

PRACTICE 1   Underline the prefix in each word. Then discuss the word's meaning with a partner. Write the meaning and an example sentence.

1. <u>dis</u>agree *to not agree: The boy disagreed with his father about the whale.*

2. impossible _____

3. invisible _____

4. unforgettable _____

5. unusual _____

6. disobey _____

PRACTICE 2

Circle the correct answer for each item.

1. The movie was _____. I can't get it out of my mind.
   a. impolite   **b.** unforgettable   **c.** impossible

2. It's too hard. It's _____ to solve this puzzle!
   a. impossible   **b.** untrue   **c.** unusual

3. 39 + 49 equals 78? No, that's _____.
   a. dislike   **b.** incorrect   **c.** invisible

4. I _____ art museums. I think they're boring.
   a. disagree   **b.** unforgettable   **c.** dislike

5. I have an _____ story to tell you. You won't believe it!
   a. incorrect   **b.** invisible   **c.** unusual

6. Some insects are so small that they are _____ to the human eye.
   a. untrue   **b.** invisible   **c.** disagree

7. Some students were _____ to the new girl in our class. I felt sorry for her.
   a. unkind   **b.** impossible   **c.** disagree

8. Not saying "thank you" is often _____.
   a. impossible   **b.** incorrect   **c.** impolite

ESSENTIAL QUESTION

Why do people see the same things differently?

First Thoughts

1. What do you see in the photo? Tell a partner.

2. Why do you think the man is playing an instrument here?

_____

_____

3. Write a title for the photo.

_____

Discuss Read the sentences about the musician in activity 1. Place an X on the line to show how possible each statement is. Then discuss your answers with a partner.

	Impossible	Possible	Very Possible
1. The musician likes playing music.	←		→
2. The musician will make a lot of money.	←		→
3. Many people will stop to listen to the musician.	←		→
4. The musician is famous.	←		→

Reading Skill: Identify the Central Idea of a Text

The **central idea** is the most important idea in a text. The central idea can be stated in a sentence, or it can be revealed through the words and phrases the author uses to discuss the topic. To identify the central idea, think about these questions:

1. What is the topic of the text?
2. What important words and ideas are included (or repeated) in the text and in the text features (title, bold words, captions)?
3. What is the most important idea the author wants you to know about the topic?

Skill in Action

Read the paragraph and a reader's thoughts. Identify the topic. Then state the central idea.

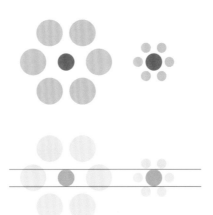

An illustration and a caption show an example of a visual illusion.

This famous visual illusion is called the Ebbinghaus illusion. It is more than one hundred years old.

Visual Illusions

Look at the two sets of circles above. Ask yourself which middle circle is bigger, the one on the left or the one on the right? Now put your finger or a pencil over each circle. Which circle is bigger now? Surprise! The circles are the same size. Don't worry if you were tricked by this **visual illusion**. It tricks most people. But how does it work? A visual illusion tricks your eyes (and brain) into seeing things differently. In this example, you think that the middle circle on the left is smaller because the outside circles are bigger.

The title is often a clue about the topic.

The phrase *visual illusion* is bolded.

I see the words *visual illusion* and *trick* repeated in the text.

This seems like an important idea.

Topic: _____

Central Idea: _____

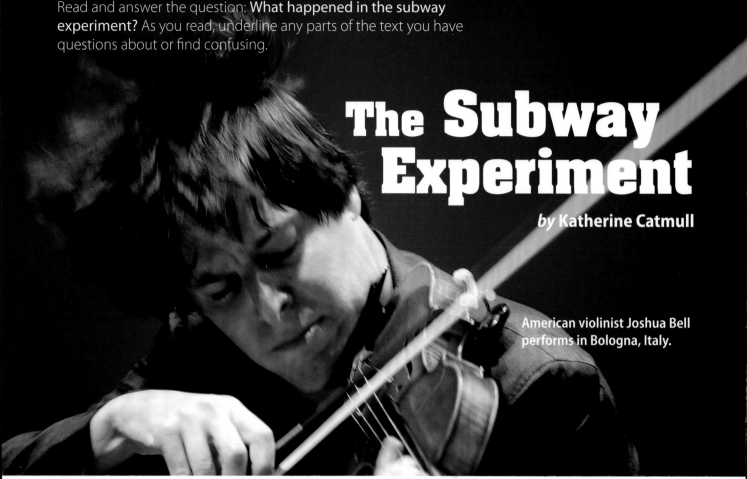

The Subway Experiment

by **Katherine Catmull**

American violinist Joshua Bell performs in Bologna, Italy.

🎧 **3.2**

1   Have you ever seen a musician in a subway or train station? Sometimes people listen and give them a little money. Most people ignore them. Now imagine it was your favorite musician that was performing. Guess what: You probably wouldn't even **notice**.

5   Oh, you **disagree**? Tell that to Joshua Bell. He's one of the most famous musicians in the world. But when he played in a Washington, D.C., subway station as part of an **experiment**, most people didn't notice.

     When Joshua Bell was four, he loved the music his parents
10   listened to. He wanted to make that music himself. So he stretched rubber bands across his dresser drawers and played them like violin strings. He even moved the drawers in and out to change the sound. His parents wondered if he would enjoy violin lessons.

     He did. Bell loved the violin and practiced for hours every day.
15   By the time he was seven, he was already an incredible musician. At seventeen, he performed for thousands of people at Carnegie Hall

> **STOP & THINK**
> **Relate** What experiences did Bell have as a child that relate to his career as a violinist?

in New York City. At eighteen, he recorded his first album. He's recorded forty more since then, many of them best sellers.

Joshua Bell has performed for a U.S. president and for British royalty. He played in the Concert Hall of the National Centre for the Performing Arts in Beijing and at the 2013 Abu Dhabi Festival. He is one of the most famous violinists in the world.

So it seems impossible, but it's true. When he played a solo concert[1] in a subway station, most people didn't stop to listen.

Usually Joshua Bell plays in concert halls with thousands of seats. These handsome halls are built to make the music sound beautiful. Tickets can cost two hundred dollars. Wearing their best dresses and suits, audience members fill up the rows of comfortable seats, ready for **entertainment**.

STOP & THINK
Describe How does the author describe concert halls?

Then the lights go down. A soft spotlight hits the stage, and Joshua Bell walks in. In black pants and a black shirt, he looks like a movie star. Whether he plays alone or with an orchestra, he uses his whole body. He works his violin with drama and passion.[2]

Most agree, watching Joshua Bell play is exciting and unforgettable. He has been called "the greatest American violinist active today." So, the audience shows him **respect**. They pay attention. They listen in complete silence. They wait until the music stops before they cough. No one wants to miss even a single note.

That's how most people see Joshua Bell perform. But in 2007, a newspaper reporter asked him to help with an experiment. What if a famous musician played in public for free? What if there was no sign saying, "Come and listen to the famous violin player!" Would people still notice the beauty of the music? Or do busy people forget to notice beauty?

Bell plays at L'Enfant Plaza Metro Station in Washington, D.C.

---

[1] **solo concert** concert with one performer
[2] **passion** strong feeling

Bell plays at the Gerald R. Ford
Amphitheater in Vail, Colorado.

50   Bell agreed to be the musician in the experiment. On a cold
January day, during the morning rush hour,[3] he stood inside the
glass doors of an unusual "concert hall": a subway station in
Washington, D.C. He wore a baseball cap and jeans. His violin case
was open for donations.[4] He began to play.

55   A cold, dirty subway station is nothing like a concert hall. The
sound echoed and bounced off hard walls. The floor rumbled[5]
as huge trains roared past below. Except for one man getting a
shoeshine, no one was sitting. Everyone was hurrying to work or
to school.

60   For the 45 minutes he played, over a thousand people passed.
Hardly anyone even looked at him. Was he invisible to them? They
didn't realize he was famous. They didn't know his violin cost
3.5 million dollars and was made in 1713 by Antonio Stradivari,
the greatest violin maker who ever lived.

STOP & THINK
Differentiate
What words does the
author use to describe
the subway station?
Are the words similar
to or different from the
words used to describe
concert halls?

[3] **rush hour**   time when many people travel to or from work
[4] **donations**   money
[5] **rumbled**   moved noisily

65 And people didn't just cough. They sneezed and chatted and talked on the phone. In between pieces, no one clapped. A few paused to buy coffee or a newspaper, but not for America's greatest violinist.

But some did stop to listen, or tried to. In fact, every child who 70 passed wanted to listen to Bell play. One three-year-old twisted and pulled at his mother's hand, trying to see the man making the incredible sounds. But he and all the other children were pulled away by busy parents.

One man walking by knew nothing about classical music. 75 He had only three minutes before he had to be at work. But he said Joshua's music "made me feel at peace." So, he waited and listened as long as he could. When he left, he dropped a few dollars in Joshua's violin case. He had never given money to a street musician before.

80 Another man, a musician himself, was working at a coffee shop. He kept peeking out to watch Bell's passionate performance. "Most people, they play music; they don't feel it," he later said. "Well, that man was feeling it."

A few other adults stopped to listen, too. Only one person 85 actually **recognized** Joshua Bell. She had attended his concert just a few weeks earlier. It was unbelievable to her, watching people throw quarters in his violin case. Just twenty-five cents for one of the greatest musicians in the world? When Bell plays in concert, he can make a thousand dollars a minute. She put $20 in his case. 90 Besides her donation, he got only $32.17.

Later, when the reporter asked people why they didn't stop, they said they were busy. They were talking on the phone. They didn't seem to notice he was there.

Joshua Bell wrote about that day, "over a thousand people 95 *heard* me play ... But very few actually *listened*."

This experiment seems to show that you might not recognize your favorite musician on the street. What do you think? Would you recognize your favorite musician? If not, would you still stop to listen?

STOP & THINK
Distinguish What is the difference between *hearing* and *listening*?

Close Read

Work with a partner.

1. Determine the meanings of your underlined words and phrases.

2. Discuss the question:

What happened in the subway experiment?

Apply the Skill: Identify the Central Idea of a Text

What is the central idea of "The Subway Experiment"? Answer the questions, and then write a sentence that states the central idea.

1. What is the topic of the text?	
2. What important words and ideas are included (or repeated) in the text and in the text features (title, bold words, captions)?	
3. Central Idea: What is the most important idea the author wants you to know about the topic?	

Understand

Read the statements. Write *T* for true or *F* for false. Then correct the false statements.

_____ **1.** Bell has been called "the greatest American violinist active today."

_____ **2.** Bell's violin was made in 1713 and cost $30.5 million.

_____ **3.** Thousands of people watch Bell play when he performs in a concert hall.

_____ **4.** Almost everyone who passed Bell in the subway stopped to listen.

_____ **5.** Bell made very little in donations during his subway concert.

Read Again and Analyze

Read the text again and respond to the questions. Use evidence from the text to support your responses.

1. **Examine** Why do you think the author explains the result of the experiment at the beginning of the text rather than at the end of the text?

2. **Compare** What is the same about Bell's performances in concert halls and his performance in the subway station?

3. **Contrast** How do most people treat Bell in a concert hall? How do most people treat him in the subway station?

4. **Give Examples** Who pays attention to Bell during his subway performance? What do they think of his performance?

5. **Infer** Why do you think Bell agreed to do the experiment?

Share Your Perspective

Discuss the questions in a small group.

1. How do you think Bell felt when people walked by him without noticing him?

2. Do you think you would notice your favorite musician playing in a subway station? Why or why not?

3. Where do you see beauty? What is beautiful to you?

Discussion Frames

I think he felt …

I think I would/wouldn't notice because …

I see beauty when …

Reflect

How does "The Subway Experiment" help you understand why people see the same things differently? Think about how people's experiences affect their perspective. With a partner, use some of the words to write sentences about the text.

Nouns	Verbs	Adverbs
concert decision entertainment experience experiment perspective reason respect	disagree notice recognize	differently

_____

_____

_____

What Do You See?

Aerial view of camels
in the desert

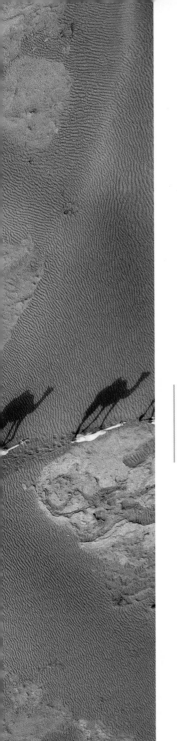

First Thoughts

Look at the diagrams. Use the words in the box to talk with a partner about how shadows are created.

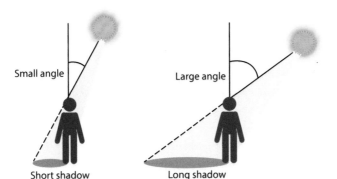

above	below
direction	light
long	shadow
short	source
sun	

Viewing Skill: Draw Important Concepts

You can remember important information in a video by drawing pictures as you watch. After you watch, you can add labels and notes to your diagram to summarize what you learned.

Apply the Skill

▶ **3.2** Use an example from the video (such as a camel or craters) to draw a picture that explains how light and shadow affect what we see. Add labels and notes.

Understand and Analyze

▶ **3.2** Watch again. Answer the questions. Support your responses with evidence from the video.

1. **Contrast** How do people's perspectives change when they see the camel picture?
2. **Explain** What is *mental rotation*?
3. **Correlate** How does the statement "It's your brain and the Sun" explain how we see shadows?
4. **Distinguish** What does the brain think when it sees a shadow at the top of an object? What about when the shadow is at the bottom of an object?

Share Your Perspective

Discuss the questions in a small group.

1. When has your brain changed how it sees an object? Maybe you saw a work of art, an optical illusion, or something that at first didn't make sense.
2. What did you see at first? What did you see after your perspective changed?

Discussion Frames

Once, I thought I saw …

Then I realized …

Reflect on the Essential Question

Think about the characters and people in this unit. What made them see things differently? Write your ideas in the idea web.

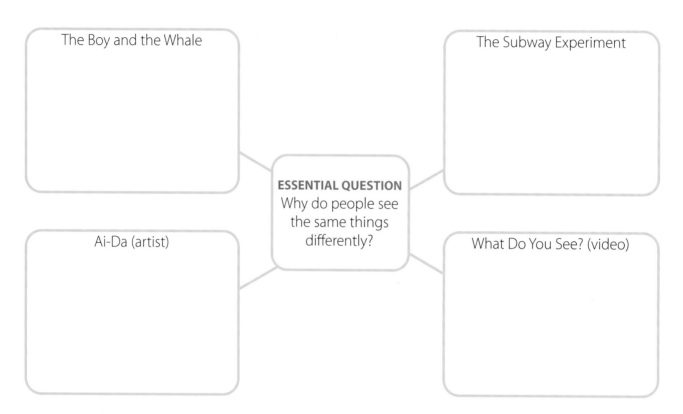

The Boy and the Whale

The Subway Experiment

ESSENTIAL QUESTION
Why do people see the same things differently?

Ai-Da (artist)

What Do You See? (video)

Discuss the Essential Question

Look at your ideas about the Essential Question earlier in the unit and your notes in the idea web above. How have your ideas about the Essential Question changed? What changed your ideas? Discuss your answers in a group.

Respond to the Essential Question

Write your response to the Essential Question.

Response Rubric
A good response will
✓ state your opinion
✓ provide support from the texts, the discussion, and your life
✓ use theme vocabulary

Theme Vocabulary

decision (n.)
differently (adv.)
disagree (v.)
experience (n.)
perspective (n.)
reason (n.)

Option 1: Write from a Different Point of View

The Boy and the Whale is written from the perspective of the boy. What if the father or the whale were telling the story? Write one scene from the story from another character's perspective. Follow these steps:

1. Complete the chart.

Point of View	
Who will tell the story?	
Motivation	
What is important to this character?	

Narration	Dialogue
What will the character see, think, or do?	What will the character say?

2. Write your scene.

3. Present your scene to a partner.

4. With your partner, compare and contrast your version of the scene with the original scene from the story.

Option 2: Host a Talk Show

Investigate the perspectives of all the participants in "The Subway Experiment" by participating in a talk show.

1. Work in a group. Have each person choose a role: the talk-show host, Joshua Bell, the reporter, Joshua Bell's mom or dad, the child who wanted to stop and listen, the woman who recognized Joshua Bell, or another person who stopped to listen.

2. Write questions on cards to ask the other talk-show participants. Give your questions to the host.

3. Take a seat on the talk-show stage. Listen as the host asks questions.

4. Answer the questions for your assigned role. Use information from the text and your own ideas to give answers.

Example:

Question (for the reporter): Why did you do this experiment?

Answer (from the reporter): I wanted to know if people are too busy to see beauty.

Assignment: Write an Argumentative Paragraph

An **argumentative paragraph** states your perspective on a topic that has more than one side. In this assignment, you will argue for one side of an argument. You can choose from the following topics or choose your own:

- *Which is better, basketball or soccer?*
- *Which is better, a beach or a mountain vacation?*
- *Which is better, remote or in-person classes?*

Your paragraph will include the following:

- a title that shows your topic
- an introductory sentence that states your argument
- three to four pieces of evidence that support your argument
- a counterargument (an opinion different from yours)
- reasons that show why you disagree with the counterargument
- a concluding sentence that summarizes your argument

Explore the Model

Read the paragraph. Look at how the writer developed his argument. What evidence supports the writer's argument? What counterargument does he use?

Language for Writing

Read the model again.

1. Circle the prepositions of place and direction the writer uses.

2. Underline the words the writer uses that contain a prefix that means "not." Write each word's definition next to it in the margin.

3. The writer uses *-ing* forms of verbs as nouns to refer to activities. Complete the sentences with the *-ing* form of the verbs in parentheses.

   You can go _____ (swim) in the water.

   You can go mountain _____ (bike) in the mountains.

   You can go _____ (ski) in the mountains.

An adventurer mountain biking in the Himalayas in Nepal

The writer states his argument in the title and in the introductory sentence. He says mountains are a good place for a vacation.

The writer includes four pieces of evidence that support his argument.

The writer includes a counterargument.

The writer includes reasons why he disagrees with the counterargument.

The writer's concluding sentence summarizes his argument.

Go to the Mountains!

The mountains are a good place for a vacation. The views from the top of a mountain are unbelievable. A vacation in the mountains is very relaxing. You can go mountain biking in the mountains. In the winter, you can go skiing. Some people think the beach is a good place to go on vacation. I disagree. The beach is incredibly hot. You can go swimming in the water, but you dive into water that is salty. When you get out of the water, you are cold. The beach is not a good place for a vacation. In conclusion, the mountains are a good place to go on vacation because of the activities you can do there.

Plan Your Writing

Complete the outline.

- Write an introductory sentence that states your argument.
- Support your argument with three pieces of evidence.
- Include a counterargument, and give reasons why you disagree with it.
- Write a concluding sentence that summarizes your argument.
- Write a title for your paragraph.

Outline

Title:	
Argument:	
Evidence: 1.	
2.	
3.	
Counterargument:	
Reasons you disagree with the counterargument:	
Concluding sentence:	

Write and Revise

Write Use your outline to write a first draft.

- Use prepositions of place or direction.
- Use words with the prefixes that mean *not*: *dis-, un-, im-,* and *in-*.

Revise Exchange argumentative paragraphs with a partner. Using the checklist, review your partner's work and give feedback. Use feedback from your partner to revise your draft.

Feedback Frames

I know what your argument is because you state …

The best evidence that supports your argument is …

You could include … as a reason why you disagree with the counterargument.

Proofread Check the grammar, spelling, punctuation, and capitalization in your argumentative paragraph. Make edits to correct any errors.

TIP Check that any difficult words you have used are spelled and used correctly, especially those with prefixes.

Publish

Share your argumentative paragraph. Read two of your classmates' paragraphs.

Present Your Argumentative Paragraph

You will present your argumentative paragraph with a visual that summarizes your evidence and counterargument.

Prepare to share your argumentative paragraph:

- Prepare a bulleted list of your evidence and counterargument reasons.
- Create a poster or computer-based presentation using your bulleted list.
- Add pictures that strengthen your argument.
- Memorize your introduction and conclusion. Use your visual to summarize your evidence and counterargument reasons.
- Practice your presentation with a partner.

Share your argument in a small group.

- Listen carefully and do not interrupt.
- After a person has shared his or her position, give feedback. To agree, you might say, "I think your evidence about … proves that …" To disagree, you might say, "I still think … is better, but I understand your point about …"

Expedition team members set up lights in Vietnam's Son Doong cave.

Son Doong Cave 🎧 3.3

EXPLORER IN ACTION
Martin Edström
is an explorer and
visual storyteller.

Edström is an explorer who specializes in creating interactive 360° videos and virtual reality (VR) documentaries. He likes to use these technologies because they help him achieve his main goal: to let viewers try on someone else's shoes. People feel like they are in the actual place when they watch his videos and VR experiences. This makes his work a great tool for helping people learn and care about important issues.

Edström has filmed interactive stories about important topics such as environmental and animal conservation. His interactive experience of Vietnam's Son Doong cave, the largest cave in the world, allow people to "walk" around the cave. Because of his work, many people around the world now know and care about the cave, and environmentalists now work to protect the cave.

▶ **3.3** Complete the sentences. Then watch the video to learn more.

1. Edström's stories feel interactive because _____

_____ .

2. Edström's stories about Son Doong are important because _____

_____

How Will You Take Action?

Choose one or more of these actions to do.

Personal

Choose to change your perspective.

1. Think of something that you have to do, such as an unpleasant chore.
2. Choose a different way to think about the task. For example, think about the benefits of doing it. Say to yourself, "I get to do this" instead of "I have to do this."
3. With a partner, discuss whether this new perspective changed your feelings.

School

Walk in your classmate's shoes.

1. Ask a partner to tell a story about a life event, such as starting a new school or getting a new pet.
2. Write a paragraph about your partner's life event. Use the first person ("I") in your story. Include details about your partner's feelings.
3. Share your story with a small group. Discuss how using "I" helped you understand his or her experience.

Local

Take pictures from different perspectives.

1. In a small group, choose different community landmarks, such as buildings or statues, to photograph.
2. Take photographs of the items from different camera angles.
3. Project your photographs for the class. Discuss what the photographs make you think or feel.

Global

Research a natural landmark.

1. Choose a natural landmark in a country that you don't know much about.
2. Prepare a two- to three-minute presentation that will convince your classmates to care about this landmark.
3. Ask your classmates if your presentation was effective.

Reflect

Reflect on your Take Action project(s). Then complete the sentences.

1. My project(s) was/were successful because _____

   _____ .

2. One thing I wish I had done differently is _____

   _____ .

3. Because of what I learned in this unit, one thing I will do is _____

   _____ .

4 Language

"Speak a new language so that the world will be a new world."
—RUMI, PERSIAN POET

What does this quote mean to you?

Look at the photo and caption. Discuss the questions.

1. What are the visitors at the museum viewing? What is on the stone?

2. Why do you think the Rosetta Stone is important?

◀ Visitors view the ancient Egyptian Rosetta Stone at the British Museum in London, England. The Rosetta Stone displays the same message in three different ancient languages.

ESSENTIAL QUESTION
What effect can words have?

Theme Vocabulary

Use these words to express your ideas throughout the unit.

PRACTICE 1 Read the conversation. Think about the meaning of each word in **bold**. Then write each word next to its definition in the chart below.

> Words can have a **positive effect** on people. In a poem, words can be beautiful and make people feel happy. Though they can also make people sad, which can have a **negative** effect.

> That's true. Words can also sometimes **cause** problems or confusion. My friends sometimes think my text messages have a negative **meaning** when I am trying to make a joke. After we **communicate** more, we can usually solve the problem.

Theme Vocabulary

cause (v.)
communicate (v.)
effect (n.)
meaning (n.)
negative (adj.)
positive (adj.)

Word	Definition
positive	relating to good instead of bad
	to exchange information using words or gestures
	relating to bad instead of good
	a change resulting from an event or action
	the thing or idea represented by words or gestures
	to make something happen

PRACTICE 2 Work with a partner. Answer the questions about the conversation.

1. What examples of the positive effects of words do the students give?
2. What examples of the negative effects of words do the students give?
3. What effects of words do the speakers agree about?

Explore the Essential Question

Think Is it easy or hard to find the right words in these situations? Check (✓) the answers that are true for you.

	Easy	Hard
talking to friends		
talking to people I don't know		
speaking another language		
writing an email		
writing a poem		
giving a presentation to an audience		

Discuss With a partner, discuss your answers to the activity above. Explain why you chose your answers.

Example: *Talking to new people is easy for me. I love meeting new people.*

Respond Circle the words that might have a positive or negative effect on someone. Add your own ideas. Then use some of the words to complete the sentences below. Share your ideas with a partner.

painful **beautiful**
communicate learn translate
share useful
meaning
useless talk
wonderful colorful
powerful message

Words can be _____ when _____.

_____ words can make you feel _____.

Key Vocabulary

PRACTICE Look at the photos and read the sentences. Discuss the meaning of the words in **bold** with a partner. Then ask and answer the questions.

collect (verb)
This woman **collects** shells.
What other things do people collect?

familiar (adjective)
Babies smile at **familiar** people, such as a parent.
Can you recognize a familiar voice on the phone?

messenger (noun)
This **messenger** is delivering a package.
What do messengers deliver in your community?

print (noun)
A bird left **prints** in the sand.
What kinds of animal prints have you seen?

shout (verb)
People **shout** when they are excited.
What are other reasons people shout?

translate (verb)
A dictionary can help you **translate** words.
Can you translate *hello* into another language?

Grammar: Relative Clauses

A **relative clause** (also called an *adjective clause*) gives more information about a noun. Relative clauses start with a **relative pronoun**, such as *who* (for people) or *that* (for people, animals, or things). The relative pronoun usually comes after the noun it refers to. The verb agrees with the noun (*words* **sound**, *the student* **writes**).

I like words *that* sound funny.

Nora is the student *who* writes poems.

PRACTICE 1 Underline each relative clause. Circle each relative pronoun. Draw an arrow from the relative pronoun to the noun it refers to.

1. I like people who are kind.

2. I study words that are hard to spell.

3. I like poets who write about love.

4. My class learns words that are useful.

5. My friend writes text messages that are really funny.

PRACTICE 2 Use all the words and phrases to write sentences with relative clauses. Use the correct form of each verb.

I have a friend	that	be exciting
She writes stories	who	sing beautiful songs
I like birds		play the guitar
I eat food		be (not) hot and spicy
We met some people		live near us

1. *I have a friend who plays the guitar.* _____

2. _____

3. _____

4. _____

5. _____

ESSENTIAL QUESTION

What effect can words have?

First Thoughts

1. Find and circle the nine words. Say each word aloud when you find it. Use a dictionary to help you, if necessary. Then answer the questions below.

Q	I	W	T	M	O	O	K	M	R	R	E
R	A	M	B	U	N	C	T	I	O	U	S
K	R	C	K	H	I	C	C	U	P	A	X
W	I	S	T	A	R	S	X	A	C	A	K
M	C	O	L	D	S	N	A	K	E	C	A
B	U	M	B	L	E	B	E	E	E	M	G
Q	C	I	N	N	A	M	O	N	Y	K	U
E	A	K	Q	Q	V	C	A	G	E	D	R

- bumblebee ✓
- caged
- cinnamon
- cold
- hiccup
- moo
- rambunctious
- snake
- stars

2. Which word is a sound (onomatopoeia) made by cows? _____

   And which is a sound made by people? _____

3. Which words are animals? _____, _____

4. Which word is a flavor? _____

Discuss Put the words from Activity 1 into categories. You can write the same word in more than one category. Then discuss your answers with a group.

Positive	Negative	Beautiful	Fun to Say

Reading Skill: Identify Theme

In a story or poem, the **theme** is the message or lesson the author wants the reader to learn. The theme might be stated in a sentence, or you may need to look more closely at the words the author uses in order to determine the theme. To identify the theme of a poem, ask yourself these questions:

1. What is the topic of the poem?
2. What details about the topic are included in the poem?
3. How does the poet think or feel about the topic?
4. What is the main message or lesson of the poem?

Skill in Action

Read the poem "Words Bounce Back" and a reader's thoughts. Think about the topic, details, thoughts, and feelings in the poem. With a partner, decide on the theme of the poem. Write it below.

The poem mentions a feeling: surprise.

The descriptive words the poet uses are negative.

These words are also negative.

Words Bounce Back

Sometimes my words bounce right back at me.
I am surprised when my words come back
dirty, sad, upset
without friends.
They smack against me, word after word,
sentence after sentence.
They don't understand what went wrong,
They only know that they are
unhappy
unwanted
lost
and so alone.
I pick them up, clean them off
and put them back in my pocket so
I can try again tomorrow.

The title can help me determine the topic. Maybe the topic is *the effect of words*.

This detail shows that even though words can have a negative effect, the speaker in the poem will try to use words again.

_____

_____

Collecting Words

by **Pat Mora**

🎧 **4.1**

1　All day, I **collect** words,
　　words that move, like *wiggle,*
　　glowing[1] words, *candle,*
　　drifting[2] words, *butterfly,*
5　　singing words, *ding-dong.*

　　I collect words that make me smile, like *tiny,*
　　that fill my mouth, *bubble* and *bumblebee,*
　　that float along, *river,*
　　that have a brown scent, *cinnamon,*
10　that sweetly stretch, *car-a-mel.*

　　I collect short, hard words, like *brick,*
　　soft words, *lullaby,*
　　cozy words, *snug,*
　　funny words, *rambunctious,*
15　scary words, *sssssssssssssnake,*
　　jumpy words, *hic-cup,*
　　big words, *onomatopoeia*—moo moo.

　　I whisper, say, **shout,**
　　　　write, and sing my words.

20　What words will you collect today?

---

[1] **glowing** shining
[2] **drifting** slowly moving

STOP & THINK
Review A stanza is a group of lines in a poem (like a paragraph in a story or an article). How many stanzas are in this poem?

STOP & THINK
Describe Poems look different from other texts. How does this poem look different from a story or an article? What is different about the punctuation?

Butterflies on a riverbank in
Tambopata National Reserve, Peru

**About the Poet
(b. 1942)**

Pat Mora is an American
poet and writer. She has
written more than thirty
books for young people
and adults. She has received
many awards for her work.

Words Are Birds

by **Francisco X. Alarcón**

🎧 **4.2**

1 words
are birds
that arrive
with books
5 and spring

they
love
clouds
the wind
10 and trees

some words
are **messengers**
that come
from far away
15 from distant lands

for them
there are
no borders
only stars
20 moon and sun

some words
are **familiar**
like canaries
others are exotic
25 like the quetzal bird

> **STOP & THINK**
> **Give examples**
> In what ways does the poet say words are similar to birds?

A quetzal on a tree branch in Monteverde Cloud Forest Biological Preserve, Costa Rica

some can stand
the cold
others migrate[1]
with the sun
30 to the south

some words
die
caged[2] —
they're difficult
35 to **translate**

and others
build nests
have chicks
warm them
40 feed them

teach them
how to fly
and one day
they go away
45 in flocks[3]

the letters
on this page
are the **prints**
they leave
50 by the sea

---

[1] **migrate** travel
[2] **caged** in a cage
[3] **flocks** groups

STOP & THINK
Recognize The first stanza on this page has five lines. How many lines are in the other stanzas on this page?

**About the Poet
(1954–2016)**

Francisco X. Alarcón was a poet and writer. He grew up in Mexico. He wrote multiple books for both young people and adults. He believed that children are "natural poets."

Collecting Words / Words Are Birds **133**

Close Read

Work with a partner.

1. Determine the meanings of your underlined words and phrases.

2. Discuss the question:

How does each poet feel about words?

Apply the Skill: Identify Theme

Complete the theme chart for "Words Are Birds."

Poem title:
Poem topic:
Details about the topic:
Thoughts or feelings shared in the poem:
Theme (message or lesson):

Understand

Read each statement and check (✓) the correct answer for Poem 1 ("Collecting Words"), Poem 2 ("Words Are Birds"), or both poems.

	Poem 1	Poem 2	Both
1. The poem compares words to birds.	☐	☐	☐
2. The poem includes examples of words that the poet likes.	☐	☐	☐
3. The poem describes different types of words.	☐	☐	☐
4. The poem describes how words grow and change.	☐	☐	☐
5. The poem shares the poet's thoughts and feelings about words.	☐	☐	☐

Read Again and Analyze

Read the poems again and respond to the questions. Use evidence from the text to support your responses.

1. **Deduce** Why does the poet of "Collecting Words" end with a question to the reader?

2. **Compare** What patterns do you see in "Collecting Words"? Are some of the lines in the poem similar? Are some words repeated in more than one line?

3. **Classify** In "Words Are Birds," does the line "some words die caged" cause a positive or negative feeling in you? Are there other lines in the poem that cause the same feeling?

4. **Examine** Birds have "no borders." How can words "cross borders"?

5. **Contrast** How are the two poems similar? How are they different?

Share Your Perspective

Discuss the questions in a small group.

1. What emotions do certain words make you feel? Give an example and explain.

2. What kinds of words would you collect? Why?

3. What other animal or object could you compare words to? Why?

Discussion Frames

Words like ... make me feel ...

I would collect words that ...

I could compare words to ...

Reflect

How do "Collecting Words" and "Words Are Birds" help you understand the effect words can have? With a partner, use some of the words to write sentences about words and language.

Nouns	Verbs	Adjectives
effect meaning messenger print	cause collect communicate shout translate	familiar positive negative

_____

_____

_____

NO WORDS

verschlimmbessern
(GERMAN)

To make something worse when you are trying to improve it

pana po'o
(HAWAIIAN)

When you scratch your head to help you remember something

depaysement
(FRENCH)

The feeling of being away from home, or being in a foreign place

ya'arburnee
(ARABIC)

When you say to someone you love that you hope you die before they do because you cannot possibly live without them

pochemuchka
(RUSSIAN)

A person who asks too many questions

chi ku
(CHINESE)

When someone can go through very difficult experiences and not become angry or unhappy

tsundoku
(JAPANESE)

When you have many books that you never read

jayus
(INDONESIAN)

When someone tells a joke that is so *unfunny* that you cannot help but laugh

Examine the Graphic

Use details from the image and the text to respond to the questions. Discuss your responses with a partner.

1. What does this graphic show?

2. What is special about each of these words or phrases?

3. Choose two or more words or phrases, and tell a partner how to say the same thing in a language that you speak. Is it possible?

Make Connections

Use details from your life, stories you've read, and the graphic to respond to the questions. Then discuss your responses with a partner.

1. Which word or phrase makes you smile? Which do you think is the funniest? The prettiest? The most interesting? Explain why.

2. Choose one of these phrases to describe a situation you have experienced. Explain the situation.

3. Do words or expressions in one language always translate into another? Why do you think this is the case?

Reflect

Use ideas from the graphic and your responses to answer the question:

What is a feeling or experience you might want to express, but do not have a word for? Make up one or more words or phrases to express it. Then share them with a partner.

_____

_____

_____

Key Vocabulary

PRACTICE Look at the photos and read the sentences. Discuss the meaning of the words in **bold** with a partner. Then ask and answer the questions.

clear (adjective)
This street sign is **clear**.
What clear signs do you see every day?

confusing (adjective)
This street sign is **confusing**.
Why is the sign in the photo confusing?

correct (adjective)
The **correct** answer to this problem is 68,894.
How many correct answers did you get on your last test?

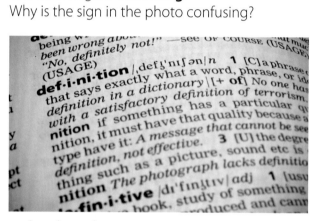

order (noun)
Dictionary words are in alphabetical **order**.
What are the names of your family members in alphabetical order?

rule (noun)
The **rule** is no cell phones in class.
What are the rules in your classroom?

switch (verb)
If you **switch** the 2 and 4 in the number 24, you get the number 42.
What new number can you make if you switch the digits in 63?

Vocabulary: Signal Words for Comparison and Contrast

Signal words for comparison connect two or more similar items or ideas.
Signal words for contrast connect two or more different items or ideas.

Signal Words	
Comparison	**Contrast**
same	different (from)
also	however
equally	instead (of)
both	although

Examples:

item 1   item 2

2 + 2 equals 4, both in France and in China.

signal word for comparison

For example, when people hear "five-and-forty," they often
write 54 instead of the correct number, 45.

idea 1

idea 2

signal words
for contrast

PRACTICE 1 Read each sentence. Circle the signal word. Then check (✔)
whether it is a comparison or contrast word.

	Comparison	Contrast
1. Both my brother and my sister have red hair.	☐	☐
2. Although most deserts are hot during the day, those same deserts can be very cold at night.	☐	☐
3. I like to drink orange juice instead of tea.	☐	☐
4. 22 is a multi-digit number. 99 is also a multi-digit number.	☐	☐
5. We don't have school on Monday. However, we still have homework.	☐	☐

PRACTICE 2 Underline the two ideas that are being compared or contrasted
in each sentence in Practice 1.

ESSENTIAL QUESTION

What effect can words have?

First Thoughts

1. What numbers do you see in the photo? Tell a partner.

2. With a partner, write the word for each number in English and in another language.

	English	Another Language
12		
19		
22		
309		

3. Look for patterns in the number words above. Circle the words you see repeated in each column. For example, is *nine* used more than once?

Discuss Check (✔) the statements you agree with. Then discuss your answers with a group.

☐ Numbers are easy to say and write in English.

☐ All languages have similar patterns for number words.

☐ Saying numbers in different languages is confusing.

Reading Strategy: Interpret Charts and Tables

Charts and **tables** include information, or data, that can be read quickly and easily. Authors use charts and tables to support the information or ideas in the text. To understand the content and purpose of a chart or table, ask yourself these questions:

1. What is the topic of the chart or table?
2. How is the chart or table labeled? What information do the labels provide?
3. Which section of the text does the chart or table support?
4. Which word, phrase, or sentence in the text explains the purpose of the chart or table?
5. How does the chart help you understand the text?

Strategy in Action

Read the paragraph from "Learning Math in Different Languages" and a reader's thoughts. Then review the chart. What is the topic of the chart? How does the chart help you understand the text?

> The text includes two examples of place value.

> The topic is the place-value rule. This sentence explains the purpose of the chart.

Multi-digit numbers follow the place-value rule. The place-value rule allows us to write any number with only ten symbols. For example, the value of the 9 in 92 is 90 (9 × 10), and the value of the 2 in 92 is 2 (2 × 1). However, in 29 it is reversed. The value of the 9 is just 9 (9 × 1), and the value of the 2 is 20 (2 × 10). This is why 92 is different from 29, although both have the same digits!

> The title helps me understand the topic of the chart.

> The chart includes seven examples of place value.

Place Value Chart for the number 4,521,392						
Millions	Hundred Thousands	Ten Thousands	Thousands	Hundreds	Tens	Ones
4	5	2	1	3	9	2

Place Value of 4 =	4000000
Place Value of 5 =	500000
Place Value of 2 =	20000
Place Value of 1 =	1000
Place Value of 3 =	300
Place Value of 9 =	90
Place Value of 2 =	2

➡ 4 5 2 1 3 9 2

> The chart labels explain the place value of each digit in the example.

Read and answer the question: **Why are some number words difficult to learn?** As you read, underline any parts of the text you have questions about or find confusing.

Learning Math
in Different Languages

by **Julia Bahnmueller, Hans-Christoph Nuerk, and Krzysztof Cipora**

1   We all do basic math. You do it. I do it. Young children do it. For instance, they do it when they count marbles. And they do it with addition. 2 + 2 equals 4, both in France and in China. 7 × 8 equals 56, both in the United States of America and in Germany.

5   Most countries use the Hindu-Arabic numeral system to write numbers. We use ten symbols to write single-digit numbers (0–9). We combine them to write multi-digit numbers (10,235).

Multi-digit numbers follow the place-value **rule**. The place-value rule allows us to write any number with only ten symbols.

10   For example, the value of the 9 in 92 is 90 (9 × 10), and the value of the 2 in 92 is 2 (2 × 1). However, in 29 it is reversed. The value of the 9 is just 9 (9 × 1), and the value of the 2 is 20 (2 × 10). This is why 92 is different from 29, although both have the same digits!

Having the same rules and symbols is great. It makes it easy

15   to talk about numbers. It almost looks like there is one math language for the whole world. You don't need to learn it again in another country. 2 + 2 equals 4, wherever you are.

The Hindu-Arabic numeral system

- includes ten symbols: 1, 2, 3, 4, 5, 6, 7, 8, 9, and 0.
- is the most common numeral system used today.

STOP & THINK
Illustrate What is the value of the 4 in 423?

Place Value Chart for the number 4,521,392

Millions	Hundred Thousands	Ten Thousands	Thousands	Hundreds	Tens	Ones
4	5	2	1	3	9	2

Place Value of 4 =	4000000
Place Value of 5 =	500000
Place Value of 2 =	20000
Place Value of 1 =	1000
Place Value of 3 =	300
Place Value of 9 =	90
Place Value of 2 =	2

→ 4 5 2 1 3 9 2

There is just one little problem. Although most of us use the same symbols to write numbers, we use very different words for these numbers. This is because we speak different languages. Look at the number words for 0–10 in Table 1. These number words differ a lot between languages. It is important for young children to know the names and the **meanings** of the numbers 0–10 in their language. And learning eleven number words is equally hard no matter what language they speak.

The number words for larger numbers can be very different in different languages. In some languages, the names for multi-digit numbers are **clear** and regular. Mandarin is one of these languages. The Mandarin number word for 29 means "two-ten-nine." The number word for 97 means "nine-ten-seven."

Scientists discovered that working with multi-digit numbers is easier for children who speak a language with clear number words. However, not all languages have clear number words. What do unclear number words look like? Look at the words for the

STOP & THINK
Compare
Which number words for the numerals 0–10 are the same or similar across languages?

	Mandarin	English	German	Hindi	
0	líng	zero	null	shuniye	0
1	yī	one	eins	ek	1
2	èr	two	zwei	do	2
3	sān	three	drei	teen	3
4	sì	four	vier	chaar	4
5	wǔ	five	fünf	panch	5
6	liù	six	sechs	cheh	6
7	qī	seven	sieben	saat	7
8	bā	eight	acht	aath	8
9	jiǔ	nine	neun	nao	9
10	shí	ten	zehn	das	10

Table 1: Number words 0–10 in different languages

number 97 in Table 2. These number words are really complicated. Other numbers are also complicated. Hindi includes a few number words that use subtraction instead of addition! For example, the number word for 29 is "unatis." It means "one before thirty" (30 − 1).

The teen numbers (11–19) are especially difficult to learn in many languages. Isn't "one-ten-two" clearer to say than "twelve" for 12? "Twelve" is a new word. "One-ten-two" uses a rule. Saying "fourteen" instead of "teenfour" is also not clear. Why do we sometimes **switch** the **order** of numbers?

> **STOP & THINK**
> **Give examples** What is an example of a clear number word? What is an example of an unclear number word?

	Mandarin	English	German	Hindi	
11	shí yī [ten one]	eleven	elf [eleven]	gyaarah [oneteen]	11
12	shí èr [ten two]	twelve	zwölf [twelve]	baarah [twoteen]	12
13	shí sān [ten three]	thirteen	dreizehn [three ten]	tehrah [thirteen]	13
16	shí liù [ten six]	sixteen	sechzehn [six ten]	saulah [sixteen]	16
17	shí qī [ten seven]	seventeen	siebzehn [seven ten]	satrah [seventeen]	17
20	èr shí [two ten]	twenty	zwanzig [twenty]	bees [twenty]	20
21	èr shí yī [two ten one]	twenty-one	einundzwanzig [one and twenty]	ikis [one and twenty]	21
29	èr shí jiǔ [two ten nine]	twenty-nine	neunundzwanzig [nine and twenty]	unatis [one before thirty]	29
48	sì shí bā [four ten eight]	forty-eight	achtundvierzig [eight and forty]	adtalis [eight and forty]	48
75	qī shí wǔ [seven ten five]	seventy-five	fünfundsiebzig [five and seventy]	chiyahatar [five and seventy]	75
97	jiǔ shí qī [nine ten seven]	ninety-seven	siebenundneunzig [seven and ninety]	sataanave [seven and ninety]	97
100	yī bǎi [one hundred]	one hundred	(ein)hundert [(one) hundred]	ek sau [one hundred]	100

Table 2: Number words greater than 10 in different languages

In English, only a few numbers (thirteen to nineteen) are switched. In other languages, such as German or Arabic, most two-digit numbers are switched. For example, in German, 97 is "siebenundneunzig." It means "seven-and-ninety." Larger numbers are even more **confusing**! The German number word for 234 means "two-hundred-four-and-thirty." The digit on the left is named first. Then the digit on the right is named. Finally, the one in the middle is named. Complicated, isn't it?

Children who speak languages with switched number words have a hard time with multi-digit numbers. German has switched number words. Japanese does not. German children make many more mistakes when they write numbers than Japanese children do. About half of the errors[1] German children make are switching mistakes. For example, when they hear "five-and-forty," they often write 54 instead of the **correct** number, 45. So a child who learns a clearer number word system has an easier time learning numbers.

234

zwei hundert vier und dreißig
(two hundred four and thirty)

We use numbers and number words every day. It is fascinating[2] to see how languages name multi-digit numbers. Although number words differ, in most cases they follow specific rules. It's something most people never think much about, but it's complicated enough to **cause** lots of errors for children learning languages with unclear number words. Once you know the facts about clear and unclear number words, 2 + 2 and 7 × 8 don't seem so basic anymore!

> **STOP & THINK**
> **Summarize** Why do German children make more mistakes when they write number words than Japanese children?

---

[1] **errors** mistakes
[2] **fascinating** very interesting

A Thai pharmacist uses a homemade abacus measuring 5.5 meters (18 feet). It may be the world's largest abacus.

Close Read

Work with a partner.

1. Determine the meanings of your underlined words and phrases.
2. Discuss the question:

   Why are some number words difficult to learn?

Apply the Strategy: Interpret Charts and Tables

Review Table 1 in the text. Answer the questions.

1. What is the table title or caption?	
2. What information do the labels provide?	
3. Which lines of the text does the table support?	
4. Which word, phrase, or sentence in the text explains the purpose of the table?	
5. How does the table help you understand the text?	

Understand

Read each statement. Write *C* for clear number words, *U* for unclear number words, or *B* for both clear and unclear number words.

1. _____ Are more complicated

2. _____ Are written with symbols

3. _____ Can be single-digit or multi-digit numbers

4. _____ Don't switch the order of numbers

5. _____ Make it harder to learn numbers

6. _____ Are the only kind of number words in Japanese

Read Again and Analyze

Read the text again and respond to the questions. Use evidence from the text to support your responses.

1. **Focus** Why is the German number word for 234 described as "complicated"?

2. **Differentiate** Which languages discussed in the article have unclear number words? Which have only clear number words?

3. **Conclude** What effect do unclear number words have on children?

4. **Relate** What should teachers know about unclear number words?

5. **Outline** What rules do the English "teen" number words (13–19) follow?

Share Your Perspective

Discuss the questions in a small group.

1. What is interesting or difficult about learning math?

2. Is math easy or difficult in the language you learned/are learning it in? Why?

3. When is math used outside of math class? Give three examples.

Reflect

How does "Learning Math in Different Languages" help you understand the effect words can have? With a partner, use some of the words to write sentences about the text.

Nouns	Verbs	Adjectives
effect	cause	clear
meaning	communicate	confusing
order	switch	correct
rule		negative
		positive

_____

_____

_____

Discussion Frames

Learning math is interesting/difficult because …

Math is easy/difficult in English/Spanish/… because …

We use math outside of math class when we …

Shakespeare's Impact on English

A Shakespeare fan celebrating his 450th birthday in Bryant Park, New York City

First Thoughts

Read the sentence that includes the phrase "have a heart of gold." With a partner, discuss the idiom. Then write a sentence or two describing someone you know who "has a heart of gold."

*My uncle **has a heart of gold**. He helps everyone in the neighborhood.*

_____

_____

Viewing Skill: Understand Key Concepts

It's important to understand the key concepts in a video. One way to do this is to identify and define important words or phrases. When you don't understand them, listen and watch for examples or definitions and note them. Determining the meaning of these key words or phrases will help you better understand the key concepts.

Example: *have a heart of gold = to be very kind, good*

Apply the Skill

▶ **4.1** Watch the video. Listen for these phrases. Write their meanings.

1. break the ice _____

2. go on a wild goose chase _____

3. see … in your mind's eye _____

4. too much of a good thing _____

Understand and Analyze

▶ **4.1** Watch again. Answer the questions. Support your responses with evidence from the video.

1. Explain Why is the knock-knock joke at the beginning of the video clever or funny?

2. Summarize What effects has Shakespeare had on the English language?

3. Deduce Shakespeare lived more than 400 years ago, but people still use his words and perform his plays. What does this tell you about language?

Share Your Perspective

Discuss the questions in a small group.

1. Which of Shakespeare's idioms reminds you of a situation you have experienced? Explain the situation.

2. What words or phrases were created in your lifetime? Where did they come from?

Discussion Frames

The idiom "…" reminds me of a time when …

An example of a new word or phrase created in my lifetime is …

Reflect on the Essential Question

Think about the material in this unit. What effect can words have? Write your ideas in the idea web.

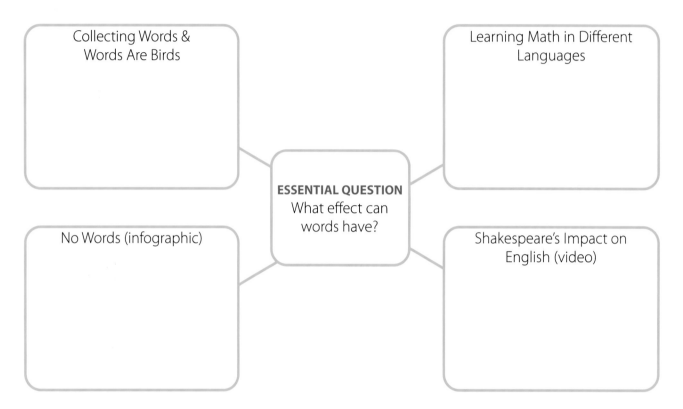

Collecting Words &
Words Are Birds

Learning Math in Different
Languages

ESSENTIAL QUESTION
What effect can
words have?

No Words (infographic)

Shakespeare's Impact on
English (video)

Discuss the Essential Question

Look at your ideas about the Essential Question earlier in the unit and your notes in the idea web above. How have your ideas about the Essential Question changed? What changed your ideas? Discuss your answers in a group.

Respond to the Essential Question

Write your response to the Essential Question.

Response Rubric
A good response will
✓ state your opinion
✓ provide support from the texts, the discussion, and your life
✓ use theme vocabulary

Theme Vocabulary

cause (v.)
communicate (v.)
effect (n.)
meaning (n.)
negative (adj.)
positive (adj.)

_____

_____

_____

Option 1: Word Art

Words can describe anything, from numbers to the people you know. In this project, you will fill an image of someone you like, love, or admire with words that describe the person.

1. Create an outline of a favorite person's face. You can do this by tracing an image you have or by turning an image into line art using a computer program.

2. Think about words that describe the person. Include words that describe how the person acts, feels, and looks. Use a dictionary or thesaurus to find new words.

3. Decide whether you will use many words or repeat only a few words on your picture.

4. Plan where the words will go on the face: hair, eyes, lips, and so on.

5. Use a pencil to draft your picture. Use a pen to finalize your picture.

6. Share your finished product with the class. Give examples of the words you used. Explain why those words describe the person.

Option 2: Play with Words

Write a sentence that uses every letter of the alphabet at least one time.

Example: *The quick brown fox jumps over the lazy dog.*

1. Write a sentence with several adjectives or adverbs.

2. Identify the letters you've used in the sentence.

3. Revise the words in your sentence until all letters of the alphabet are included.

4. Read your sentence to a partner. Check that you have a subject and a verb and that the grammar and punctuation are correct.

5. Count the letters in each of your sentences. Determine which one of you used the fewest number of letters in your sentence.

Assignment: Write a Poem

Poetry is a type of literature that connects to people's thoughts and feelings. In this assignment, you will write a poem that includes your thoughts and feelings about words, language, or numbers.

Your poem should have at least ten lines and include the following:

- a title that connects to the theme and content of the poem
- at least two stanzas
- your thoughts and feelings about words, language, or numbers
- at least two relative clauses

Explore the Model

Read the model. Look at how the poet organized the poem and developed a theme. Then answer the questions.

1. How many stanzas are there? _____ How many lines? _____

2. What is the theme of the poem?

_____

Language for Writing

Read the model again.

1. Underline the relative clauses in stanzas 2–4. Circle the relative pronouns at the beginning of each relative clause.

2. The writer includes several examples for each type of word she likes. List the words that belong to each group.

Words from Other Languages	Soft, Cozy Words	Long, Important Words

3. Look at the example of alliteration in the model. Write words from another line in the poem that repeat the *r* sound.

r: _____, _____, _____

Friends having ice cream with a view of the Charles Bridge in Prague, Czechia

The poet connects the title to the theme of the poem.

The poet organizes the poem into four stanzas.

The poet uses relative clauses to give more information.

The poet lists examples of the words.

The poet uses alliteration, which is the repetition of sounds at the beginning of words. For example, *dance, daintily,* and *down.*

Word Love

I like words that are translated
Zmrzlina, which is Czech for ice cream
Sirimiri, which is Spanish for a very light rain
Nakakapagpabagabag, which is Tagalog for causing worry

I like soft, cozy words that make me feel safe
Words like *sheep, sleep,* and
seashore

I like long, important words that make me look smart
Words like *advanced, colleague,* and
diploma

I like poets who write beautiful words
Words that dance daintily down the page
Words that make my heart run and race rapidly
I like poets who make me cry
Even when I don't understand all their words

Plan Your Writing

Complete the outline.

- Decide on the words, languages, or numbers that you want to write about.
- Include examples of words that belong in each group.
- Select words and ideas that support your theme.
- Add a title that connects to the theme and content of your poem.

Outline

Title:		
Theme (What message or lesson do you want your readers to learn?):		
Group 1:	Group 2:	Group 3:
Examples of words:	Examples of words:	Examples of words:

Write and Revise

Write Use your outline to write a first draft.

- Use relative clauses to describe the groups of words and your theme.
- Try using alliteration, or repeating the sounds at the beginning of words.

Revise Exchange poems with a partner. Using the checklist, review your partner's work and give feedback. Use feedback from your partner to revise your draft.

Feedback Frames

I like the stanza about …

You could add examples such as … and … to support your ideas.

I like how you express the theme in the line about …

☐ Does the writer include a title?

☐ Does the writer describe his or her thoughts and feelings about words, languages, or numbers?

☐ Does the writer connect his or her thoughts and feelings to examples of words, languages, or numbers?

☐ Does the writer include at least ten lines and two stanzas?

☐ Does the poem have a theme? What is it?

Proofread Check the poem for accidental spelling and punctuation errors. Make edits to correct those errors.

Publish

Share your poem. Read two of your classmates' poems.

TIP

Check that you've written your poem in lines and stanzas. Check that your relative clauses start with the correct relative pronoun.

Present Your Poem

You will recite your poem. When you recite a poem, you read it with emotion or expression.

Prepare to share your poem:

- Underline the words in the poem that you want to read with feeling. Decide which emotions to express as you read. (Will you read the words with a happy voice, a sad voice, or another emotion?)
- Decide where you will pause as you read. Poets usually pause at the end of each idea instead of at the end of each line.
- Share your poem in a small group.
- Listen carefully to each person's poem.
- After each person has shared his or her poem, give positive feedback. You might comment on the specific words in the poem, the theme, or the feelings that the person expressed.

TAKE ACTION

Linguist K. David Harrison (right) with Abamu Degio (left) and Anthony Degio (center), speakers of the endangered language Koro

Exploring Language 🎧 4.4

EXPLORER IN ACTION
K. David Harrison is a professor of linguistics.

About half of the world's 7,000 languages will disappear in the next 100 years. Without these languages, we lose not only words, but also important knowledge about the world. K. David Harrison and other linguists record, translate, and study conversations of endangered languages. This helps them understand not only the words and grammar, but also a community's values and knowledge. For example, the Inuit people have more words for sea ice than scientists do. This tells linguists that sea ice is important to the Inuit people and they can describe it better than most people in the world. Documenting their language helps us better understand the natural world they live in. Recording dying languages will help ensure that we do not lose information about the world.

▶ **4.2** Answer the questions. Then watch the video to learn more.

1. Harrison studies languages in order to _____

_____.

2. If we lose a language, we also lose _____

_____.

How Will You Take Action?

Choose one or more of these actions to do.

Personal

Collect words important to your culture.

1. Think about how your culture is different from other cultures.
2. Brainstorm three to five words that represent these differences.
3. Use pictures and symbols to illustrate your words on a poster. Present your words to a small group and explain their cultural importance.

School

Survey language use.

1. Conduct a survey to determine how many languages students in your school speak. Include questions about when and for what purpose they speak each language.
2. Distribute the survey to each class.
3. Have a small group present the results of the survey.

Local

Share the poems and stories of local writers and storytellers.

1. Find someone in your community who likes to write poetry or tell stories.
2. Ask that person, "What kinds of words do you like to use in your poetry/stories?"
3. In class, present a poem or story written by the person, and summarize the feelings he or she shared about language.

Global

Research an endangered language.

1. Identify a language with few speakers in your country or in a part of the world you are interested in.
2. Research the language. Identify why the language is dying and how many speakers are left. Learn a few words of the language.
3. Share the information you learned with your class.

Reflect

Reflect on your Take Action project(s). Then complete the sentences.

1. My project(s) was/were successful because _____

   _____

2. One thing I wish I had done differently is _____

   _____

3. Because of what I learned in this unit, one thing I will do is _____

   _____

5 Determination

"A journey of a thousand miles begins with a single step."

—LAO ZI,
CHINESE PHILOSOPHER

What does this quote mean to you?

Look at the photo and caption. Discuss the questions.

1. Describe the photo. Have you ever surfed? Do you want to?

2. How does a sport like surfing require determination?

◄ **Surfer Mike Coots, who lost his leg to a shark attack when he was 18, surfing in Kauai, Hawaii**

ESSENTIAL QUESTION

What makes someone determined?

Theme Vocabulary

Use these words to express your ideas throughout the unit.

PRACTICE 1 Read the conversation. Think about the meaning of each word in **bold**. Then write each word next to its definition in the chart below.

> What is a **goal** you have? How **determined** are you to reach it?

> I want to score over 90% on my math test. I'm determined to meet this goal. I work hard. Sometimes I get tired and want to **give up**, but I don't. I take a break and then **continue** to work. One **obstacle** is finding time to study and do my chores. But if I am **successful** at reaching this goal, my parents will let me get a pet.

Theme Vocabulary

continue (v.)
determined (adj.)
give up (v. phr.)
goal (n.)
obstacle (n.)
successful (adj.)

Word	Definition
goal	something you are trying to do or achieve
	feeling strongly that you are going to do something and that nothing will stop you
	to keep doing something
	achieving what you want
	to stop doing something
	something that makes it difficult to make progress or move ahead

PRACTICE 2 Work with a partner. Answer the questions about the conversation.

1. What is the student's goal?
2. How will he reach his goal?
3. Why is he determined to reach his goal?

Explore the Essential Question

Think What is a goal you have? Why are you determined to reach your goal?

1. Write a sentence or two to describe a goal you have and why you are determined to reach it.

   Example: *One goal I have is to study zoology. I am determined to reach my goal because I want to be a veterinarian.*

   _____

   _____

2. Think about your goal. Check (✓) the ideas that are true for you. Then add your own idea to the list.

   I show that I am determined by …

   ☐ working on my goal for weeks or months.

   ☐ continuing to work on my goal even when there are obstacles.

   ☐ completing difficult tasks that are part of my goal.

   ☐ not giving up when I want to stop.

   ☐ believing I will be successful.

   ☐ _____ .

Discuss With a partner, discuss activities 1 and 2 above.

Respond Circle the words related to the word *determined*. Add your own ideas. Then use some of the words to complete the sentence below. Share your ideas with a partner.

be the best   work hard
excited   nervous
win   happy   determined
help someone   frustrated   sad   strong
make my parents proud

When you are determined, you might feel _____ because you want to _____ .

Key Vocabulary

PRACTICE Look at the photos and read the sentences. Discuss the meaning of the words in **bold** with a partner. Then ask and answer the questions.

audience (noun)
This **audience** is watching a play.
Do you think this audience is enjoying the play?

cheer (verb)
The people are **cheering** at a soccer game.
What do you do when you cheer for someone?

disaster (noun)
His cake burned. It is a **disaster**.
What are other examples of disasters?

excitement (noun)
You can see **excitement** on their faces.
What is the reason for their excitement?
Make a guess.

perform (verb)
This group **performs** music all over the world.
Do you like to perform in front of people?

nerves (noun)
This girl is controlling her **nerves**, though it isn't easy. When is it difficult to control your nerves?

Vocabulary: Understand Similes and Onomatopoeia

Good writers use a wide variety of words or phrases to help readers understand a text. Writers can use:

- a **simile:** a phrase with *like* or *as* that compares two things
- **onomatopoeia:** words that sound like the sounds they describe

Examples:

Ojiichan would play a lullaby so soothing that sleep would fall over her like a blanket.

> The author compares sleep to the feeling of a blanket. This phrase is a **simile**.

She pulled at the strings, letting them twang. It was true that she was still a beginner.

> The verb *twang* is an example of **onomatopoeia**. It sounds like the noise you hear if you pull a violin string.

PRACTICE 1 Read the sentences from the text. Circle the correct type of language for each underlined word or phrase.

1. She practiced in front of her dog, Jojo, who cocked his head and sometimes <u>growled</u> at the strange sounds Hana made.

    a. simile   **b.** onomatopoeia

2. Hana squared her shoulders and took her violin and bow inside, leaving her brothers laughing <u>like monkeys in the tree.</u>

    a. simile   **b.** onomatopoeia

3. As Hana continued to play all the special sounds she had practiced, the air around her came alive with <u>buzzing</u> bees…

    a. simile   **b.** onomatopoeia

4. Ojiichan played every morning. From his study, the clear, bright notes would drift upstairs, … and coax her awake <u>as gently as sunshine</u>.

    a. simile   **b.** onomatopoeia

PRACTICE 2 Circle the meanings that make the most sense for the similes and onomatopoeia from Practice 1.

1. The dog *growled* at Hana, which means her violin playing sounded *good / bad*.

2. Laughing at Hana "like monkeys in the tree" means that Hana's brothers probably thought her violin playing was *good / bad*.

3. The "buzzing bees" in the air around Hana mean Hana *kept / stopped* making sounds.

4. Ojiichan's music woke up Hana every morning "as gently as sunshine," which means it was *very nice / upsetting* to wake up that way.

ESSENTIAL QUESTION

What makes someone determined?

First Thoughts

1. What do you see in the photo? Tell a partner.
2. What is the boy feeling and thinking? Write your ideas.

_____

_____

_____

_____

_____

3. Write a title for the photo.

_____

Discuss Read the sentences. Check (✔) the box that best describes you. Then discuss the questions below with a partner.

How do you feel when you perform?		
☐ I'm really scared.	😖	I'm a disaster. I want to give up when I see the audience. I can't talk or think.
☐ I'm nervous.	😳	I don't like to perform. I can control my nerves, but I'm still nervous!
☐ I'm excited.	😁	I love the excitement of performing! I love when people clap and cheer for me.

1. Which one best describes you? Why?
2. In *Hana Hashimoto, Sixth Violin*, you will read about a beginning violin player who performs for an audience for the first time. How do you think she may feel about performing?

Reading Skill: Analyze Character

Authors write strong stories by creating interesting characters. Characters often face problems or obstacles. To better understand a character, ask yourself these questions:

1. What problems and obstacles does the character face?
2. How does the character respond? Find details in the text about the character's thoughts, actions, or feelings.
3. What do the character's responses tell you about the character?

Skill in Action

Read the excerpt from *Hana Hashimoto, Sixth Violin* and a reader's thoughts. What do you learn about Hana? Complete the chart below.

> These details describe Hana's problem and some of the obstacles.

> Additional details tell more about her obstacle.

When Hana Hashimoto announced that she had signed up for the talent show and that she would be playing the violin, her brothers nearly fell out of a tree.

"That's just loopy," said Kenji. "You're still a beginner."

"Stop kidding," said Koji. "You can barely play a note."

"It's a talent show, Hana."

"You'll be a disaster!"

Hana squared her shoulders and took her violin and bow inside, leaving her brothers laughing like monkeys in the tree.

She pulled at the strings, letting them twang. It was true that she was still a beginner. She had only been to three lessons.

> At the beginning of the story, I learn that Hana wants to play violin in a talent show.

> Hana responds. She stands up straight and walks away. I can analyze these actions to understand what Hana is like.

Analyze Character	
Obstacle	Hana has only had _____ violin lessons.
Obstacle	Her brothers _____ she can play well.
Character's response	"Hana squared her shoulders" shows that Hana is _____ _____ .
Your opinion of Hana (with evidence)	Hana is _____ . I know this because _____ _____ .

Read and answer the question: **What do Hana's brothers think of her violin playing at the beginning, middle, and end of the story?** As you read, underline any parts of the text you have questions about or find confusing.

Hana Hashimoto, Sixth Violin

by **Chieri Uegaki**

🎧 **5.1**

1   When Hana Hashimoto announced that she had signed up for the talent show and that she would be playing the violin, her brothers nearly fell out of a tree.

"That's just loopy," said Kenji. "You're still a beginner."

5   "Stop kidding[1]," said Koji. "You can barely play a note."

"It's a talent show, Hana."

"You'll be a **disaster**!"

Hana squared her shoulders and took her violin and bow inside, leaving her brothers laughing like monkeys in the tree.

10   She pulled at the strings, letting them twang. It was true that she was still a beginner. She had only been to three lessons.

---

[1] **kidding** joking

The first time Hana held a real violin had been that summer, while visiting her grandfather in Japan.

Long, long ago, her grandfather had been part of a great
15 symphony orchestra in Kyoto. Ojiichan had been Second Violin and once played in front of the Imperial Family.[2]

Ojiichan played every morning. From his study, the clear, bright notes would drift upstairs, through the shoji[3] screen doors to where Hana slept on sweet-smelling tatami[4] mats, and coax her
20 awake as gently as sunshine.

Hana always asked for a song about a crow cawing for her seven chicks. Whenever Ojiichan played it, Hana would feel a shiver of happy-sadness ripple through her.

Ojiichan didn't just play songs. He could also make his violin
25 chirp like the crickets Hana tried to find in the tall grasses.

He could pluck the strings to mimic the sound of raindrops on the oil-paper umbrella Hana twirled under during summer storms.

And when the first fireflies[5] emerged at twilight, Ojiichan could compose a melody that seemed to make them dance higher
30 and glow brighter than ever before.

---

[2] **the Imperial Family** the family of the Japanese emperor
[3] **shoji** sliding
[4] **tatami** straw
[5] **fireflies** insects that produce a flashing light

STOP & THINK
Sequence Did Hana visit Japan before or after she signed up to be in the talent show?

At the end of each day, as Hana lay with her head resting on a cool buckwheat pillow, Ojiichan would play a lullaby so soothing that sleep would fall over her like a blanket.

On their last day together, Hana told Ojiichan that she wanted
35 to learn to play the violin. And when Hana got home, her parents agreed that she could.

Now Hana was practicing not just for lessons, but for the talent show, too.

Hana practiced every day, just like Ojiichan. And every day, her
40 brothers fled[6] the house with covered ears, complaining about the horrible noise.

She practiced in front of her parents, who listened with care while they washed and dried the dishes.

She practiced in front of her dog, Jojo, who cocked his head
45 and sometimes growled at the strange sounds Hana made.

And she practiced on her own, in front of an old photo of Ojiichan from his symphony days. Alone, Hana could pretend she was **performing** in front of an **audience** so appreciative they called for encore after encore.[7]

50 The day of the talent show arrived, and the school auditorium thrummed with **excitement**. Backstage,[8] Hana waited with a walloping heart. A dozen acts, including five other violinists, had already gone before her.

> **STOP & THINK**
> **Deduce** Why does Hana perform in front of a photo of Ojiichan?

---

[6] **fled** ran from
[7] **encore after encore** extra performance after extra performance
[8] **backstage** behind the stage

Finally, Hana heard the master of ceremonies call her name.

55 As Hana walked onto the stage, her violin tucked under her arm and bow gripped tight in her hand, an oceanic roar filled her ears.

Things seemed to be moving in slow motion, and for one dizzy moment, Hana thought, "Kenji and Koji were right. This is going 60 to be a disaster." She wished she could turn into a grain of rice and disappear into a crack between the floorboards.

She could hardly see with the spotlight in her eyes. Yet as Hana looked out into the audience, certain faces appeared to her, as if through a telescopic lens.[9]

65 She could see her brothers, melting into their seats.

She saw her best friend, Jas, giving her two thumbs up.

And there, her smiling mother, and her father, camera in hand.

Hana held a breath, then ballooned her cheeks before letting 70 it out. With a whoosh, the roaring in her ears receded. Then, as everyone seemed to disappear beyond the light shining down on her like a moonbeam, she remembered.

"*Gambarunoyo Hana-chan.*" Do your best, her grandfather had told her. Ojiichan would be **cheering** for her.

---

[9] **telescopic lens** piece of curved glass that makes things look larger and brighter

75   Hana swallowed her **nerves** like medicine and leaned toward the microphone. She would just do her best.

"This is the sound of a mother crow calling her chicks," she said. She placed the violin under her chin, held her bow in position and played three raw, squawky notes.

80   "This is the sound of my neighbor's cat at night." She dragged the bow across the strings, and the violin yowled in loud protest.

"This is the sound of rain on a paper umbrella." Hana plucked the strings for a soothing *plomp-plomp-plomp*.

As Hana **continued** to play all the special sounds she had
85   practiced, the air around her came alive with buzzing bees …

… and lowing cows

… and squeaking mice

… and croaking frogs.

Finally as the last sound effect trailed away, Hana tucked
90   her bow and violin under her arm. "And that," she said to the audience, "is how I play violin."

Then she took a great big bow.

> **STOP & THINK**
> **Summarize** What does Hana play for the audience?

Later, after dinner, Kenji surprised Hana by asking for an encore. "Make that funny cow sound again," he said.

95   Then Koji said, "Make that crazy cat sound, too."

So Hana did. And when her mother and father and brothers all laughed, she happily played her sounds again.

    Perhaps next year Hana would be able to perform one of Ojiichan's favorite pieces. But for now, Hana played a little melody

100 she had been practicing, remembered from nights lit by dancing fireflies. She imagined that the notes would drift out through the window, past the bright rabbit moon and beyond, and Ojiichan would hear them and smile.

About the Author (b. 1969)

Chieri Uegaki is the author of *Suki's Kimono, Ojiichan's Gift, Rosie and Buttercup,* and *Hana Hashimoto, Sixth Violin.* Her books have received the Ezra Jack Keats Book Award and a Governor General's Award nomination. Chieri lives on the Sunshine Coast in British Columbia, Canada.

Close Read

Work with a partner.

1. Determine the meanings of your underlined words and phrases.
2. Discuss the question:

   What do Hana's brothers think of her violin playing at the beginning, middle, and end of the story?

Understand

Read the summary. Cross out the mistakes and correct them.

During the summer, Hana visited her grandfather, Ojiichan, in Japan. Ojiichan was a great violin player. Ojiichan's music made Hana feel ~~energetic~~ *happy* and sad. At home, Hana asked to take violin lessons. She took ten lessons. Then she decided to enter a talent show. Her brothers thought it was a good idea. She practiced every day. On the day of the talent show, Hana waited backstage. She was excited. She thought of her grandfather's words: "Don't give up." She played different animal sounds. After the performance, her brothers said her violin playing was a disaster.

Read Again and Analyze

Read the text again and respond to the questions. Use evidence from the text to support your responses.

1. **Infer** Why does Hana want to play the violin?
2. **Contrast** Reread lines 46–49. How does Hana feel when she imagines she is performing for an audience? How is this different from her feelings when she sees the audience at the talent show?
3. **Examine** Reread lines 39–49. Why does the author include four paragraphs about Hana practicing the violin?
4. **Infer** Reread lines 51–53. How does Hana feel when she is waiting backstage?
5. **Deduce** Is Hana's performance a success? Why or why not?

Apply the Skill: Analyze Character

Complete the chart to analyze how Hana responds to events in the story.

Story Event	Hana's Response (an action, thought, or feeling)	What do Hana's responses tell you about her?
Hana's parents agree that she can learn the violin.		
Hana's brothers leave the house when she practices.		
Hana gets scared when she walks on stage.		

Share Your Perspective

Discuss the questions in a small group.

1. When does Hana feel the most determined to play the violin? When does she feel the least determined?
2. Think of a goal that you have had. When did you feel most determined to reach your goal? When did you feel least determined to reach it?

Discussion Frames

Hana is most/least determined when …

One goal I had was …

I was most/least determined when …

Reflect

How does *Hana Hashimoto, Sixth Violin* help you understand what makes people determined? With a partner, use some of the words to write sentences about the story.

Nouns	Verbs	Adjectives
audience disaster excitement goal nerves obstacle	cheer continue give up perform	determined successful

_____

_____

_____

Garrett Morgan: Determined to Save Lives

Morgan improved traffic safety by inventing a new type of traffic light.

Garrett Morgan, American inventor (1877–1963)

First Thoughts

What problem does each object solve? Which is the most useful or important, in your opinion?

turn signal

oxygen mask

life jacket

Understand and Analyze

▶ **5.1** Watch the video. Answer the questions. Support your responses with evidence from the video.

1. **Identify** What is one thing Morgan invented? How did it help to protect people?
2. **Summarize** Describe the events that lead to the rescue of the men in the mine.
3. **Infer** Considering his two inventions, what words might describe Morgan's personality?
4. **Illustrate** How was Morgan creative? Give an example.

Viewing Skill: Understand Anecdotes

When you watch a video, listen for **anecdotes**, or short stories, that the speaker uses to make a point. Think about why the speaker tells this story. What does it help you understand? How is it connected to the ideas in the video?

Apply the Skill

▶ **5.2** Watch the excerpt. Circle the correct words and phrases.

… Morgan noticed that when the elephants needed fresh air, they would poke their trunks through an opening at the *top / bottom* of the tent and take a breath. This gave him a great idea. He could attach breathing tubes to his smoke hood! Morgan knew that in a fire, smoke *rises / falls*, and there is cleaner air *above / below*. He added tubes to his mask that reached toward the *sky / ground*.

Share Your Perspective

Discuss the questions in a small group.

1. What might make you determined to invent something?
2. If you could make an invention to save people's lives, what would it be?

Key Vocabulary

PRACTICE Look at the photos and read the sentences. Discuss the meaning of the words in **bold** with a partner. Then ask and answer the questions.

believe (verb)
The runner **believes** she can win the race.
What do you believe about yourself?

frustrated (adjective)
The student is **frustrated** because the assignment is unclear.
When are you frustrated?

impossible (adjective)
The mountain looks **impossible** to climb.
What other tasks seem impossible?

selfless (adjective)
Firefighters are **selfless**. They take risks to help others.
What are other examples of selfless actions?

task (noun)
Our **task** is to rake the leaves.
What are tasks you do at home or at school?

tease (verb)
The girl's classmates **tease** her.
How does she feel?

Grammar: Simple Past Tense

We use the simple past tense to talk about actions that started and ended in the past.

Regular Verbs		
We add -ed to the end of most verbs to form the simple past tense. Here are rules for other verbs.		
Spelling Rules	**Present**	**Past**
If the verb ends in e, just add -d.	tease	tease**d**
If the verb ends in a consonant + y, change the y to i and add -ed.	try	tr**ied**
If a one-syllable word ends in a vowel + consonant, double the consonant and then add -ed.	stop	sto**pped**
Irregular Verbs		
Some verbs are irregular. For irregular verbs, we don't add -ed to form the simple past tense. Their word form changes: He **sells** wood. (present) He **sold** wood. (past)		
have → had make → made do → did is/are → was/were		

PRACTICE 1 Read the paragraph from "The Mountain Man of Gehlour."
Complete the sentences with the simple past tense form of the verb in parentheses.

As a young man, Dasrath Manjhi ____married____ (marry) a
woman named Falguni Devi, and the couple _____ (have)
a son. Life in Gehlour _____ (is) difficult, and Dasrath
_____ (work) hard to support his family. He
_____ (raise) goats. Sometimes he _____ (chop)
down trees and _____ (sell) the wood; other times he
_____ (help) farmers.

PRACTICE 2 Read the text, and underline the irregular simple past tense form of
the verbs listed below. Then write the simple past tense forms.

Dasrath's heart <u>was</u> broken. Frustrated and angry, he knew
he had to do something. "That mountain had shattered so many
pots, claimed lives. I could not bear that it hurt my wife," he later
said. "If it took all my life now, I would carve us a road through
the mountain." So began a task that seemed impossible.

begin _____   know _____   is ____was____

say _____   take _____   has _____

ESSENTIAL QUESTION

What makes someone determined?

First Thoughts

1. What do you see in the photo? Tell a partner.

2. What do you think the people might say to each other? Write a conversation.

_____

_____

_____

_____

3. Write a title for the photo. _____

Discuss Check (✓) the statement you most agree with. Then discuss your answer with a group.

☐ People are most determined when their goal is to help others.

☐ People are most determined when they want to do something for themselves, like climb a mountain.

☐ People are most determined when their task seems impossible.

☐ People are most determined when they are frustrated and want to change something.

Reading Strategy: Visualize

Good readers use words from the text to **visualize**, or create pictures in their minds. When you visualize, you "see" the people and events in the text. To visualize, ask yourself these questions:

1. What do the places and people look like? Look for words that tell the color, size, or shape.

2. What do the people do? Look for verbs that describe how the people move and what they do.

3. What can you hear, smell, taste, or touch from the story?

After you read a paragraph, close your eyes and imagine you are in the story.

Strategy in Action

Read the paragraph from "The Mountain Man of Gehlour" and a reader's thoughts. Underline the words that the reader uses to visualize.

> I see a group of small houses at the bottom of a mountain. Outside the homes, there are clothes hanging to dry.

Dasrath Manjhi was born and raised in the small village of Gehlour in northeastern India. The village was one of the poorest in the country. It was located near a steep and rocky mountain. People of the village had no schools for their children. They had no hospital and no electricity. They did not even have a market for food, and often ate snails, roots, or rats. For a doctor and other services, villagers would travel 70 kilometers around the bottom of the mountain to a larger town on the other side. The trip around the mountain could take two days.

> I see a high mountain. The mountain looks like a wall made of rock.

> On the other side of the big mountain, I see a large town. There are many more buildings. There is a hospital and schools. The town is busy with people.

> Behind the houses, I see people digging in the dirt. I can smell the wet dirt as they dig up the plants for food.

The Mountain Man of Gehlour

by Elizabeth Massie

"The Mountain Man of Gehlour" tells the true story of Dasrath Manjhi, (1929–2007).

🎧 **5.2**

1   Everyone has problems and **obstacles** during their lives. Some obstacles are small while others seem to be "as big as a mountain." Dasrath Manjhi faced

5   an obstacle that wasn't just as big as a mountain, it was an actual mountain!

Dasrath Manjhi was born and raised in the small village of Gehlour in northeastern India. The village was one of the poorest

10 in the country. It was located near a steep and rocky mountain. People of the village

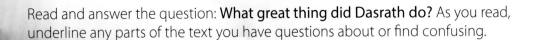

had no schools for their children. They had no hospital and no electricity.[1] They did not even have a market for food, and often ate snails, roots,[2] or rats. For a doctor and other services, villagers
15   would travel 70 kilometers around the bottom of the mountain to a larger town on the other side. The trip around the mountain could take two days.

       Why didn't the people of Gehlour just hike over the mountain rather than go around it? Some did, but the trip was dangerous.
20   The path was narrow and rough. Climbing over the mountain made the distance shorter, but it wasn't safe. People had been hurt or had died as they tried to cross. And so, the people of Gehlour could not easily get many of the things they needed.

       As a young man, Dasrath Manjhi married a woman named
25   Falguni Devi, and the couple had a son. Life in Gehlour was difficult, and Dasrath worked hard to support his family. He raised goats. Sometimes he chopped down trees and sold the wood; other times he helped farmers tend[3] their crops in fields near and far from home. It was backbreaking work, but Dasrath was used to it.

30   One day in 1959, Dasrath was working on the other side of the mountain. Falguni left home to take a pot of food to her husband. Rather than hiking around the mountain, she climbed a path up and along the side of the unsafe, rocky ridge. She struggled not to fall as stones rolled beneath her feet.
35   Suddenly, her foot twisted. The pot of food flew from her hands, and she fell, badly hurting her leg. When Dasrath found her, he was upset

---

[1] **electricity** energy used to power lights and machines
[2] **roots** underground parts of plants
[3] **tend** take care of

STOP & THINK
Deduce What do you think life is like for people in Gehlour compared to life in the larger town?

STOP & THINK
Visualize Imagine you are watching a movie of the events. How do you feel watching Falguni climb the mountain?

and worried. He knew her injury was serious. He took her home, but she became very ill. Unable to travel the distance to a doctor in time, Falguni died.

Dasrath's heart was broken. **Frustrated** and angry, he knew he had to do something. "That mountain had shattered so many pots, claimed[4] lives. I could not bear that it hurt my wife," he later said. "If it took all my life now, I would carve[5] us a road through the mountain." So began a **task** that seemed **impossible**.

He sold his goats to buy a hammer and chisel. Then, each day, Dasrath worked in the fields, and each evening, he took his tools up the mountain to carve a road. Hour after hour, day after day, he chipped through the stone, carting off the chunks of rock that fell.

A road through the mountain? His fellow villagers thought Dasrath's **goal** was ridiculous! They **believed** he was wasting his time and energy trying to punish the mountain for taking Falguni. But every day, Dasrath hiked farther into the mountain and chopped off a little more and then a little more.

Week after week, month after month, year after year, Dasrath hammered at the mountain. He quit his job to work on the road all day and night. He often went without food. At one point, he even moved his house closer to the mountain to save time. He was very tired but never **gave up** on his dream. The villagers **continued**

---

[4] **claimed** took
[5] **carve** cut

to laugh. They did not believe Dasrath would be **successful**. They said he was crazy for trying to cut through the mountain, but that only made him more **determined** to reach his goal.

Finally, the people of the village began to understand Dasrath's determination. They saw that nothing would stop him, and they no longer **teased** him. Some began to help by bringing him food, water, and tools as he continued to cut away the rocks. Now, instead of calling him crazy, they called the roadbuilder "Baba," which means "wise old man." They also called him the "Mountain Man."

Dasrath worked on the road for 22 years. In 1982, the impossible became possible. The road was finished! There was now a safe route across the mountain. The trip was shortened from 70 kilometers to about 3. At last, the villagers of Gehlour were able to more quickly reach doctors, schools, and goods.

Dasrath wasn't done, however. He wanted the road to last, so with the help of others, he paved[6] the road. When finished, he said, "I started this work out of love for my wife, but continued it for my people. If I did not, no one would." Dasrath Manjhi's amazing mountain road still exists today, and although he died in 2007, Gehlour's **selfless** "Mountain Man" is remembered with great respect.

_____

[6] **paved** covered with stone or concrete

STOP & THINK
Explain The villagers teased Dasrath. What effect does their laughter have on him?

STOP & THINK
Paraphrase Quotation marks appear around the words that Dasrath said. In your own words, explain why he built the road.

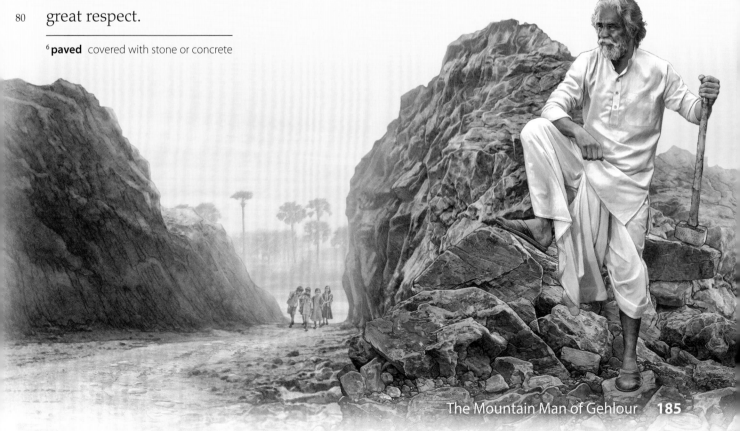

Close Read

Work with a partner.

1. Determine the meanings of your underlined words and phrases.
2. Discuss the question:

   What great thing did Dasrath do?

Apply the Strategy: Visualize

Find the lines in the text. Reread the details. Then write what you visualize.

The text says ...	I see ... I hear ... I smell ...
(Lines 25–29) Life in Gehlour was difficult, ... but Dasrath was used to it.	
(Lines 31–37) Falguni left home to ... and she fell, badly hurting her leg.	
(Lines 63–66) Finally, the people of the village ... and tools as he continued to cut away the rocks.	

Understand

Circle the words to complete the sentences. Then number the events in the order that they appear in the story (1–4).

_____ Dasrath began the seemingly *impossible* / *easy* task of digging through the mountain. His *goal* / *obstacle* was to build a road.

_____ Falguni *fell* / *gave up* while climbing the mountain and died because the hospital was far away.

_____ After 22 years, Dasrath was *successful* / *frustrated*. Finally, there was a road through the mountain.

_____ At first, people *believed* / *teased* Dasrath. But this only made him more *frustrated* / *determined*.

Read Again and Analyze

Read the text again and respond to the questions. Use evidence from the text to support your responses.

1. **Recognize** Why is the mountain an obstacle? What problems did the mountain cause for the people of Gehlour?

2. **Identify** Name three obstacles Dasrath faced.

3. **Illustrate** What do the villagers believe about Dasrath at the beginning of his task and at the end? Give examples to show their thoughts.

4. **Deduce** Why does the author describe Dasrath as "selfless"?

5. **Infer** The people of Gehlour could now travel to the town more quickly. How else did the road through the mountain change their lives?

Share Your Perspective

Discuss the questions in a small group.

1. Dasrath believed in his dream. Other people didn't believe in it, but Dasrath never gave up. How does it feel when people question your dreams? What do you do?

2. What three details from the story do you think best show Dasrath's determination?

3. How do you feel about Dasrath? Why do you think the author told Dasrath's story?

Discussion Frames

When people don't believe in my dream, I feel …

I think the details that best show his determination are …

I think the author told this story because she wanted people to understand that …

Reflect

How does "The Mountain Man of Gehlour" help you understand what makes people determined? With a partner, use some of the words to write sentences about the story.

Nouns	Verbs	Adjectives
goal obstacle task	believe continue give up tease	determined frustrated impossible selfless successful

_____

_____

_____

Examine the Photo

1. Look at the photo. Describe what you see.
2. How do you think this photo shows determination?
3. Write 3–5 questions about the photo. Discuss your questions with a small group.

Find Out ▶ 5.3

Watch photographer Renan Ozturk talk about his photo.

1. Did he answer any of your questions? Which ones?
2. How many months did it take Ozturk and Andy to get this photo? What were some of their obstacles?
3. Ozturk says that taking this photo took a "lifetime." What does he mean?

Reflect

Renan Ozturk was determined to take this photo. How were his reasons or actions similar to or different from Hana Hashimoto's or Dasrath Manjhi's?

Share Your Story

Share a photo in a group.

1. Take a photo of the same outdoor place at different times of the day over several days. Note the time, weather, and other information.
2. Note any obstacles you faced.
3. Choose the best photo. Share it and information about it with your group.

ABOUT THE PHOTOGRAPHER

Renan Ozturk is an adventure photographer and filmmaker who has explored many parts of the world.

Reflect on the Essential Question

Think about how the people and characters in this unit showed determination.
What made each person determined? Write your ideas in the idea web.

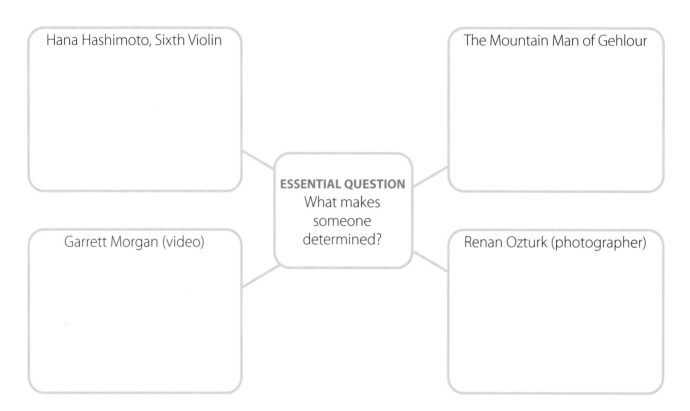

Hana Hashimoto, Sixth Violin

The Mountain Man of Gehlour

ESSENTIAL QUESTION
What makes someone determined?

Garrett Morgan (video)

Renan Ozturk (photographer)

Discuss the Essential Question

Look at your ideas about the Essential Question earlier in the unit and your
notes in the idea web above. How have your ideas about the Essential Question
changed? What changed your ideas? Discuss your answers in a group.

Respond to the Essential Question

Write your response to the Essential Question.

Theme Vocabulary

continue (v.)
determined (adj.)
give up (v. phr.)
goal (n.)
obstacle (n.)
successful (adj.)

Response Rubric
A good response will
✓ state your opinion
✓ provide support from the texts, the discussion, and your life
✓ use theme vocabulary

_____

_____

_____

Option 1: Write a Poem

Write a poem about an important event from "The Mountain Man of Gehlour" or *Hana Hashimoto, Sixth Violin*. Then read it to your classmates. Use similes and onomatopoeia to describe Manjhi as he carves a path or Hana as she practices or performs.

Example:

Hana Plays for Everyone

Hana plays for her brothers.
Squawk! Squeak! Is she playing the violin
    or a chicken?
Hana's brothers yowl with laughter.
Squeak! Twang! She is only a beginner.
Zip! Her brothers race across the room. *Bam!* They
    slam the door.
Hana plays for her dog. The dog leaves the room as
    quietly as a mouse.
Hana plays for her parents.
Swish! They dry the dishes. Their smiles are like
    sunshine.

Option 2: Make a Short Video

Make a short video about a character from a movie or a book who is determined to reach a goal.

1. Make a plan for your video. What images will you show? What will you say?

	I will show . . .	I will say . . .
What is the name of the character and the movie or book?		
What is the movie or book about?		
How is the character determined to reach a goal?		

2. Make your video.

3. Post your video to a class website.

4. Watch three of your classmates' videos and give feedback. You can say, "I like the detail about . . ." or "I can tell the character is determined because . . ."

Assignment: Write a Personal Narrative

A **personal narrative** tells a story from your life. In this assignment, you will write a paragraph about a time you were determined to complete a difficult task. You will describe the events and your thoughts and feelings.

Your personal narrative will include the following:

- a title that shows what you were determined to do
- a sentence that tells the setting (where and when the events happened)
- a description of the events that happened before, during, and after you completed the difficult task
- sentences that share your feelings during the events
- a sentence that concludes the story

Explore the Model

Read the model. Look at how the writer developed her personal narrative. How does she conclude it?

Language for Writing

Read the model again.

1. Circle descriptive words that help you visualize the events. Underline phrases that show the writer's feelings.

2. Find the simple past tense verbs. Write at least five regular and five irregular simple past verb forms in the chart.

Regular Past Tense Verbs	Irregular Past Tense Verbs

3. The writer uses the phrase "wanted to" to tell what she was determined to do. Complete the sentences with the verbs from the model:

I wanted to _____ my writing.

I wanted to _____ Mr. Lang my talent.

The title gives clues about what the writer was determined to do. —————•

The setting is a school classroom. The writer doesn't say this. She uses details to show it. —————•

This signal word helps the reader follow the sequence of events. —————•

This descriptive verb helps the reader understand how the writer feels. —————•

These details show that the writer is nervous. —————•

This last sentence concludes the story. —————•

Finding My Voice

The bell rang and I slid into my seat. I opened my folder and took out my poem. I wanted to read it, but I was scared. What would people think? First, Mr. Lang called on Maria. She read her poem and the class cheered. I liked the sound of the words. Next, another student read aloud. This time, I couldn't listen. I said the words of my own poem in my head. My heart pounded. I could hear it thundering in my ears. But I knew I could do it. I wanted to share my writing. I wanted to show Mr. Lang my talent. I raised my hand. My voice squeaked. It didn't sound like me. I paused. Someone laughed. I caught my breath and began again. The words came out slowly. I made my voice loud. Then I reached the end. The class was quiet. Finally, I raised my eyes and looked at Mr. Lang. He smiled, and the sound of clapping filled the room.

Plan Your Writing

Complete the outline.

- Complete the sentences to describe a time you were determined to complete a task.
- Describe what happened before, during, and after the task.
- Write details to show how you felt.
- Write a title that shows what you were determined to do.

Outline

Title:
I was determined to: I wanted to do this because: The time and place was:
Before the task: How I felt:
During the task: How I felt:
After the task: How I felt:

Write and Revise

Write Use your outline to write a first draft.

- Use descriptive words to help the reader visualize the events.
- Use signal words to help the reader: *First, Next, Then, Finally.*

Revise Exchange personal narratives with a partner. Using the checklist, review your partner's work and give feedback. Use feedback from your partner to revise your draft.

Feedback Frames

You did a nice job showing …

I think your narrative could use more descriptive verbs / details / signal words …

☐ Does the writer tell the setting?

☐ Does the writer clearly describe the sequence of events?

☐ Does the writer share his or her feelings?

☐ Does the writer use descriptive words to help you visualize?

☐ Does the writer conclude the story?

Proofread Check the grammar, spelling, punctuation, and capitalization in your narrative. Make edits to correct any errors.

TIP Check that you've used the correct simple past tense form of each verb. Underline the past tense verbs. Check the spelling of regular and irregular verbs.

Publish

Share your personal narrative. Read two of your classmates' narratives.

Present Your Personal Narrative

You will retell your personal narrative. When you retell a story, you don't read it. You use notes or say it from memory.

Prepare to share your personal narrative:

- Underline the sentences in your paragraph that show your determination.
- Make short notes of the events and feelings so you can retell them without reading.
- Practice retelling your story to a partner.

Share your personal narrative in a small group.

- Listen carefully and do not interrupt.
- After a person has shared his or her story, give feedback. You might say "That was an amazing story. I like how you …"

A mobile dinosaur museum
making a stop in rural Mongolia

Protecting Mongolia's Fossil Heritage 🎧 5.3

EXPLORER IN ACTION

Bolortsetseg Minjin, Ph.D., is a paleontologist. She founded the Institute for the Study of Mongolian Dinosaurs (ISMD).

Many important dinosaur fossil discoveries have been made in the Gobi Desert in southern Mongolia. The Gobi Desert is the largest dinosaur reservoir in the world. More than 80 different types of dinosaurs have been discovered there, including the velociraptor. In the past, paleontologists from outside of Mongolia made these discoveries. Now Mongolian paleontologist Dr. Minjin is determined to teach Mongolians about the country's important fossil history, to help other Mongolians become paleontologists, and to promote dinosaur tourism.

Dr. Minjin founded the Institute for the Study of Mongolian Dinosaurs in 2007. Many people in Mongolia don't know about the important fossil discoveries made in their country. The institute spreads knowledge about Mongolia's fossil history and builds interest in paleontology. It also protects fossils from being removed from Mongolia. Many of the institute's programs teach young people about Mongolian dinosaurs and fossils. Since 2013, the institute has supported a movable dinosaur museum. Dr. Minjin believes that projects like these will increase the number of Mongolian paleontologists and better protect Mongolia's rich fossil heritage.

▶ **5.4** Complete the sentences. Then watch the video to learn more.

1. Mongolia is an important paleontology site because _____

_____

2. One goal of Dr. Minjin's institute is _____ .

How Will You Take Action?

Choose one or more of these actions to do.

Personal

Show determination to reach a goal.

1. Choose a goal, such as getting a better grade in a difficult class.
2. Think of steps to reach your goal. Write them on a calendar.
3. List a few obstacles. How can you overcome the obstacles? Discuss your ideas with a partner.

School

Honor determined students or staff members.

1. Take photos of students or staff and staff members working hard in your school.
2. Write short captions. Explain how determination helped them succeed.
3. Exhibit the photos in your school.

Local

Raise money for a cause you believe in.

1. Find an organization in your town that works hard to do something you care about.
2. With your classmates, find a way to raise money for the organization. For example, hold a car wash fundraiser.
3. Deliver the money to the group with a thank-you card or video.

Global

Learn about protected sites.

1. Research a protected site, such as the Flaming Cliffs in the Gobi Desert, that is located in a different country.
2. Write a paragraph that shares details about the site and why it needs to be protected. Add your own ideas about how to further protect the site.
3. Share your paragraph with your classmates.

Reflect

Reflect on your Take Action project(s). Then complete the sentences.

1. My project(s) was/were successful because _____

   _____.

2. One thing I wish I had done differently is _____

   _____.

3. Because of what I learned in this unit, one thing I will do is _____

   _____.

6 Becoming Me

"Your wings already exist; all you need to do is fly."

—MAHA AL BALUSHI, OMAN'S FIRST FEMALE PILOT

What does this quote mean to you?

Look at the photo and caption. Discuss the questions.

1. What is the girl in the photo doing? What do you think her interests are?

2. Describe or show a photo of yourself that shows your interests.

◄ **A tourist poses for a photo at the Bund, a waterfront district in Shanghai, China.**

ESSENTIAL QUESTION
How do I become who I want to be?

Theme Vocabulary

Use these words to express your ideas throughout the unit.

PRACTICE 1 Read the conversation. Think about the meaning of each word in **bold**. Then write each word next to its definition in the chart below.

> What do you want to be when you **grow up**?

> I want to be a concert piano player like the **talented** Lang Lang. He played piano at the 2008 Beijing Olympics. People all over the world love his music. He's my **inspiration**. And you? What do you want to be?

> I'm not sure. My family wants me to be a doctor, but I have different **interests**. I love art and drawing. Should I follow my dream and be an artist? Or should I **become** a doctor? I don't know how to **decide**.

Theme Vocabulary

become (v.)
decide (v.)
grow up (v. phr.)
inspiration (n.)
interest (n.)
talented (adj.)

Word	Definition
become	to begin to be or come to be something
	to make a choice about something
	a feeling of wanting to learn more about something or to be involved in something
	a person, place, or experience that makes someone want to do or create something
	to become an adult
	having a special ability to do something well

PRACTICE 2 Work with a partner. Answer the questions about the conversation.

1. What interests do the students have?

2. Which student discusses his or her inspiration? What is the inspiration?

3. How can the students decide their futures? What advice do you have for them?

Explore the Essential Question

Think How do people decide what they want to do? Read the profiles below. Underline a sentence that shows each person's interest or inspiration.

Muhammad Yunus saw poor women in Bangladesh selling furniture. The women needed money for their materials, but banks would not loan money to them. Muhammad started a bank to help them. His bank has helped 7.5 million people.

Zahra Lari saw a movie called *The Ice Princess* when she was 10 years old. Because of it, she wanted to become an ice skater. Zahra woke up very early so she could use the one rink in Abu Dhabi before the hockey players. Zahra hopes to be the first UAE ice skater at the Winter Olympics.

Dong Zhiming is a Chinese paleontologist. He studies dinosaurs and is one of the best people in the world at finding their fossils. He first saw a dinosaur fossil at a museum when he was thirteen years old. That day had a big impact on the rest of his life!

Discuss With a partner, compare the sentences you underlined. Then discuss your inspiration.

Respond Circle the words related to becoming who you want to be. Add your own ideas. Then use some of the words to complete the sentence below. Share your ideas with a partner.

decisions   **family**
early experiences   interests
talent   **inspiration**   change the world
hard work
think for myself   skills   **school**
culture
language
stories
values   friends

These things have the biggest impact on who you will become:

_____ and _____ .

Key Vocabulary

PRACTICE Look at the photos and read the sentences. Discuss the meaning of the words in **bold** with a partner. Then ask and answer the questions.

chance (noun)
They wanted the **chance** to share their thoughts.
What do you want the chance to do?

discover (verb)
She **discovered** some ancient coins.
Have you ever discovered something you didn't expect?

invent (verb)
Scientists **invented** a robot that can move like a human.
What do you want to invent?

require (verb)
Airlines **require** you to show photo identification.
What does your teacher require you to do each day?

thoughtful (adjective)
He was **thoughtful** before his next turn.
When are you thoughtful?

training (noun)
His pilot **training** lasted for three months.
What other jobs need special training?

Grammar: Possessive Nouns and Adjectives

Possessive Nouns

We use **possessive nouns** to show that a noun (often a person) owns something. Add an apostrophe and -*s* (*'s*) to the noun.

Example: *Everyone liked* **Ben's** *bike. (Ben has a bike. The bike belongs to Ben.)*

Rule	Example
If the noun is singular, always add *'s*.	**Carla's** idea
If the noun is plural and ends in *s*, only add an apostrophe (*'*).	the **boys'** bedroom
If the noun is plural and does not end in *s*, add *'s*.	the **children's** toys

PRACTICE 1 Use the noun in parentheses to complete each sentence with a possessive noun.

1. _____ house is on Market Street. (Mr. Patel)
2. _____ chocolate cake is delicious! (Luis)
3. My _____ bike-rental business is very successful. (family)
4. The _____ soccer game is on Tuesday. (men)
5. The _____ drawings were very good. (students)

Possessive Adjectives

We also use **possessive adjectives** (*my, our, your, her, his, its, their*) to show possession.

Examples:

I have a brother. **My** *brother is* **my** *best friend.*

We have a car. **Our** *car needs repairs.*

You have a sister. **Your** *sister is smart.*

He/She/It has a problem. **Her/His/Its** *problem is difficult to solve.*

They have chores. **Their** *chores are easy to do.*

PRACTICE 2 Complete each sentence with the correct possessive adjective.

1. Susan is a talented artist. _____ paintings are so beautiful.
2. Carlos is a thoughtful student. _____ ideas are always interesting.
3. My parents own a restaurant. _____ restaurant is very busy on the weekends.
4. You had an essay to write and math problems to do. Did you finish all _____ homework?
5. I want to become a scientist. _____ hope is to invent new ways to travel to space.

ESSENTIAL QUESTION

How do I become who I want to be?

First Thoughts

1. What do you see in the photo? Share your ideas with a partner.

2. Write three sentences to create a story about the photo. Tell what is happening. Use two of the words from the box.

chance	discover	interest	invent	require	thoughtful	training

_____

_____

_____

3. Write a title for the story. _____

Discuss Write answers to the questions. Share them in a small group. Then try to find answers that everyone in the group shares. Circle the answers you have in common.

	Questions	**Answers**
Talents	What are you good at?	
Interests	What do you love to do or learn about?	
Inspiration	Who do you want to be like?	
Skills	What skills do you have?	

Reading Strategy: Make Text-to-Self Connections

When you make connections, you use what you know to help you understand the text. A **text-to-self connection** is a connection between your life and the text. To make a connection, read part of the text, and then pause and ask yourself the following questions:

- What does this remind me of in my own life?
- Has something like this ever happened to me?
- How am I similar to the character(s) in the story?

Strategy in Action

Read the paragraphs from *Rickshaw Girl* and a reader's connections. What do the connections help the reader understand? What connections can you make to your life? Then discuss with a partner.

This reminds me of learning to skateboard. It was very fun when I started moving. I was surprised. I couldn't believe I was doing it! I understand Naima's excitement.

I remember when I was on my skateboard. I was going fast down a hill. It was so scary. My heart was pounding. I didn't know how to stop. This helps me understand that Naima is very scared.

Naima glanced around. The village was silent; the lane empty. Quickly she climbed up on the cycle seat. Grasping the handles for balance, she pressed hard with her feet.

The rickshaw[1] started rolling downhill.

She was doing it! She was driving the rickshaw.

As she turned the pedals, Naima pictured Father's smile as she handed him the *taka*[2] she had earned.

Before she realized what was happening, the lane began to curve at the bottom of the slope. Desperately Naima tried to turn the rickshaw, but she couldn't seem to change directions. She squeezed the hand brakes as hard as she could, but the rickshaw seemed to pick up speed instead of slowing down. She couldn't stop it.

CRASH! The rickshaw just kept hurtling through the thicket like a stampeding animal.

I remember when I was in a chess match. I pictured my dad smiling with happiness when I won. I understand that Naima wants to make her dad happy.

[1] **rickshaw** small, covered vehicle with two wheels
[2] **taka** form of money used in Bangladesh

Read and answer the questions: **How would you describe Naima? What does she want to do?** As you read, underline any parts of the text you have questions about or find confusing.

excerpts from
Rickshaw Girl

by **Mitali Perkins**

1 **Naima**

Naima raced through her morning chores, trying hard to be careful.

Mother smiled. "Well done, Naima. You may wait outside
for Father."

5 Naima went quickly to the flat, wide stone just outside the
doorway of their hut. Most of the homes in the village looked the
same, with smooth clay walls, thatched roofs, dirt paths, and large
stone thresholds.[1] They only looked different on holidays, when girls
decorated their family's paths and thresholds with painted patterns
10 called *alpanas*, just as their ancestors[2] had done for generations.[3]
In Naima's village, on International Mother Language Day, when the
whole country celebrated the beauty of their Bangla language, the
leaders gave a prize to the girl who painted the best alpanas.

Humming under her breath, Naima carefully mixed up a batch
15 of rice-powder paint. She'd **invented** a new pattern of curves, lines,
and squares in her mind while doing her chores. Before she started
painting, she had to wipe off her last practice design. "Stop and
think before you act," Mother often reminded her. But she never
needed to warn Naima to be **thoughtful** when it came to
20 painting alpanas.

> **STOP & THINK**
> **Infer** How does Naima
> feel about painting
> alpanas? How do
> you know?

---

[1] **thresholds** gates, doors
[2] **ancestors** past members of the family
[3] **for generations** over decades or centuries

Father's Rickshaw

Naima glanced around. The village was silent; the lane empty. Quickly she climbed up on the cycle seat. Grasping the handles for balance, she pressed hard with her feet.

25 The rickshaw[4] started rolling downhill.

She was doing it! She was driving the rickshaw.

As she turned the pedals, Naima pictured Father's smile as she handed him the *taka*[5] she had earned.

Before she realized what was happening, the lane began to
30 curve at the bottom of the slope. Desperately Naima tried to turn the rickshaw, but she couldn't seem to change directions. She squeezed the hand brakes as hard as she could, but the rickshaw seemed to pick up speed instead of slowing down. She couldn't stop it.

35 CRASH! The rickshaw just kept hurtling through the thicket like a stampeding animal.

The thorns had captured Father's gleaming new rickshaw, bushes closing around it like a trap.

---

[4] **rickshaw** small, covered vehicle with two wheels
[5] *taka* form of money used in Bangladesh

STOP & THINK
Predict In this excerpt, Naima is driving her father's rickshaw. Why do you think she is driving it?

Naima's Idea

40　　One day Father surprised them by coming home early for lunch. "The rickshaw's looking worse than ever," he said. "It's starting to rust. And Hassan's shop should be open for business by now. I'll go there today, and if it's open, I'll price the repairs."

　　"But … have you earned enough money, Father?" Naima
45　asked, even though she knew the answer.

　　The idea came wheeling into her mind as though it had been waiting for the **chance**. She was still the best alpana painter in the village, wasn't she? Surely painting rickshaws wasn't much harder than designing alpanas. Why couldn't she work for the rickshaw
50　painter in exchange for the rickshaw repair?

STOP & THINK
Summarize What problem is Naima trying to solve? What is her idea?

The Rickshaw Repair Shop

　　"Excuse me," Naima said politely, coming up behind the woman. "Is this Hassan's Rickshaw Repair Shop?"

　　"What do you want? Can't you see that I'm busy?"

55　　"My father's rickshaw needs repairs," she answered. "I came to see if I could do some work in exchange for them. May I see the repairman to ask him this favor[6]?"

　　"I *am* the repairman," the woman said.

　　Naima's head whirled and her mouth fell open. This widow[7]
60　was the owner of a rickshaw repair shop? Here—in a village just like her own? How could that be? But the woman had half-turned to see her, and that was a brush in her hand.

STOP & THINK
Deduce In this excerpt, Naima is visiting a repair shop. Why does her mouth "fall open"?

---

[6] **favor** kind act
[7] **widow** woman whose husband has died

RICKSHAW REPAIR SHOP

"My first order, and only one day to complete it," the woman
was saying, almost as if she were talking to herself. "I need to
concentrate, and all I get are interruptions."

"I could help you," Naima said suddenly. "I paint the best
alpanas in my village."

The woman sighed but didn't stop painting. "Are you still
here?" she asked. "Why don't you go and bother someone else?
We both know that boys don't paint alpanas."

Naima took off her cap and let her braid tumble down.
"I'm not a boy," she said.

The woman's brush stopped in midair. "A-re!" she said, looking
as amazed as Naima must have when Naima had **discovered** her
identity. "Why are you dressing up like that, then?"

The story poured out of Naima like water from a pitcher.
"… and it was all my fault," she ended. "I can't earn money
because I'm a girl, so I borrowed these clothes."

"Who says girls can't earn money?" the woman asked. She
adjusted her saree, folded her arms across her chest, and jutted
out[8] her chin.

"I don't know who made the rule," Naima answered. "But it's
always been like that."

"Things are changing whether people around here like it or
not. These days a woman who wants to start her own business can

STOP & THINK
Make Connections
When have you been
told you couldn't do
something? How did
you feel?

---

[8] **jutted out** stuck out

borrow money from our women's bank. We **decided** to put our money together and help each other."

As she listened Naima caught sight of an old-fashioned rickshaw. It was freshly painted with borders of orchids and lilies
90 and water hyacinths outlining each panel. Something about the borders that decorated each panel reminded Naima of an alpana design.

Meanwhile the rickshaw woman was studying Naima's hands. "Hmm," she said thoughtfully. "I *could* use some help—Ali won't
95 give me more business if I don't finish by tomorrow, even if he is family. Painting a rickshaw panel from scratch[9] **requires** a lot of **training**, but I might let you try touching up one of the panels that still looks somewhat decent."

Taking a deep breath, Naima squatted in front of the panel.
100 She chose a clean brush and dipped it into the pot of orange. She gripped the brush firmly, just as the woman did, and started painting. It wasn't hard to follow the original painter's lines. She brightened the yellow stripes on the tiger's fur. With a wider brush she splashed blue across the pond, making it sparkle like the one
105 on the back of Father's rickshaw.

[9] **from scratch** from the beginning

STOP & THINK
Infer How do you think Naima will earn money?

About the Author
Mitali Perkins was born in Calcutta, India, and grew up in Ghana, Cameroon, England, Mexico, and the United States. She believes that stories are spaces where young people "feel safe, welcome, and beloved." Her strong characters inspire readers all over the world.

Close Read

Work with a partner.

1. Determine the meanings of your underlined words and phrases.

2. Discuss the questions:

   How would you describe Naima? What does she want to do?

Apply the Strategy: Make Text-to-Self Connections

What text-to-self connections did you make as you read the story? Add two.
Then tell what they help you understand.

The text says …	This reminds me of …	This helps me understand …
(Lines 46–47) *The idea came wheeling into her mind as though it had been waiting for the chance.*	*This reminds me of when I had a difficult math problem. At first, I couldn't figure it out. Then suddenly I had the answer. I knew what to do!*	*I understand that Naima is excited. She thinks she has solved the problem. She figured out how to help her dad.*

Understand

Write *Naima*, *The rickshaw woman*, or *Father* to complete the sentences.

1. _____ owns and usually drives the rickshaw.

2. _____ drove the rickshaw and crashed it.

3. _____ is the owner of the repair shop.

4. _____ paints beautiful alpanas and is very talented.

5. _____ discovers Naima is hiding who she is.

6. _____ borrowed money from a bank.

7. _____ gives Naima the chance to work.

Read Again and Analyze

Read the text again and respond to the questions. Use evidence from the text to support your responses.

1. **Infer** Why does Naima try to drive the rickshaw? Was your prediction the same as your current answer?

2. **Examine** Why does Naima dress as a boy?

3. **Deduce** How did the woman become the owner of Hassan's Rickshaw Repair Shop?

4. **Characterize** What words best describe the repair shop owner? Give examples to support your response.

5. **Compare** How are Naima and the owner of the shop similar?

Share Your Perspective

Discuss the questions in a small group.

1. What effect do you think the owner of the repair shop will have on Naima's life?

2. If you had the chance to get special training, what kind of training would you get? Why?

3. What do young people require in order to become who they want to be?

Discussion Frames

One effect on Naima's life may be that she …

If given the chance, I would get training for …

In order to become who they want to be, young people require …

Reflect

How does *Rickshaw Girl* help you understand how to become who you want to be? With a partner, use some of the words to write sentences about the story.

Nouns	Verbs	Adjectives
chance	become	talented
inspiration	decide	thoughtful
interest	discover	
training	grow up	
	invent	
	require	

_____

_____

_____

LOUIS BRAILLE

" We must be treated as equals— and communication is the way we can bring this about. "

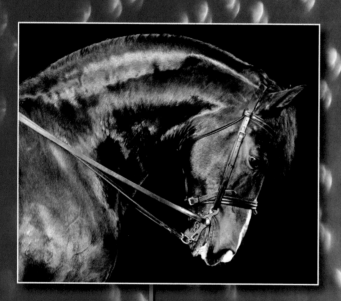

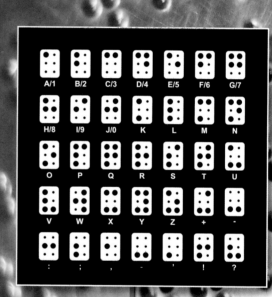

1809–12	1812	1812–19	1819	1821	1824
Born in Coupvray, France, Louis Braille spent his early years playing in his father's workshop. His father made harnesses for horses.	At the age of 3, he hurt his eye while playing with his father's tools. After an infection, he became completely blind.	He attended school in Coupvray. His parents encouraged him to do things other children were doing.	At age 10, he was able to attend one of the first blind schools in the world, the National Institute for Blind Children in Paris.	He learned a writing system by a man named Barbier, called "night writing." Barbier created the system of raised dots for soldiers to read in the dark.	At age 15, Braille came up with an improved system of raised dots that represent the alphabet. The system let blind people read and write more easily.

Examine the Graphic

Use details from the graphic to respond to the questions. Discuss your responses with a partner.

1. What kinds of events does the graphic show? How is the information organized?

2. What caused Braille to become blind?

3. How did Braille's parents treat him? What effect do you think this had?

4. Describe how the Braille writing system works.

5. Identify two important events and the effect they had on Braille's life.

Make Connections

Use details from your life, stories you've read, and the graphic to discuss your responses with a partner.

1. What are experiences that many people have as they grow up?

2. What do you think defines a person, or makes them who they are?

Reflect

Use ideas from the graphic and your responses to answer the question:

What kinds of events are life changing?

Give examples to support your response.

> **Discussion Frames**
>
> In my opinion, life-changing events are events that cause you to …

1826

He graduated at age 17 and became a teacher at the National Institute for Blind Children.

1829

He published the first book describing his system, now known as Braille. It was not widely used until after his death.

1852

He died of tuberculosis at the age of 43. His system is now the standard way for blind people to communicate.

Key Vocabulary

PRACTICE Look at the photos and read the sentences. Discuss the meaning of the words in **bold** with a partner. Then ask and answer the questions.

culture (noun)
Food is a big part of Chinese **culture**.
What other things are part of one's culture?

encourage (verb)
They **encouraged** her to finish the race.
How do you feel when someone encourages you?

expect (verb)
He **expects** to do well on his driving test.
What do you expect to do well on?

form (verb)
He invited other students to **form** a study group.
What other groups do students form?

knowledge (noun)
She has a lot of **knowledge** about space.
What do you have a lot of knowledge about?

original (adjective)
Her fashion is **original**.
What do you think is another word for *original*?

Vocabulary: Use a Dictionary

Use a dictionary to find the definition of a word, to check its pronunciation, to confirm its part of speech, and to see it used in an example sentence. Follow these steps to look up a word from the text in the dictionary:

1. Find the word in the dictionary.

2. Some words have more than one entry. Locate the entry that matches the part of speech of the word from the text.

3. Read the definitions. Then reread the text with the word. Find the definition in the dictionary that best matches the use of the word in the text.

4. Read the example sentence from the dictionary to confirm you have the correct part of speech and definition.

Example:

The dancers practiced hard to <u>perfect</u> the moves. Finally, they were ready.

Main entry Pronunciation
Part of speech Definitions are numbered Example comes after the definition

perfect *adj.* /ˈpʌrfɪkt/ **1** the best possible: *a perfect score* or *record* ‖ *If only the world were perfect!* **2** complete and faultless, with nothing wrong or missing: *This car is in perfect condition.* **3** appropriate and satisfactory in every respect: *The holiday decorations were perfect.* **4** total, complete, thorough: *a perfect fool* ‖ *a perfect stranger*

v. /pərˈfɛkt/ to make flawless, excellent: *She perfected her style of playing the piano by practicing several hours a day.*

There are two entries for *perfect* in the dictionary. *Perfect* in the example sentence above is a verb and matches the meaning and example for the second entry.

PRACTICE Use the dictionary entries above. Circle the correct answer.

1. Which part of speech matches the meaning of *perfect* in this sentence?

   I want to **perfect** my language skills so everyone can understand me.

   a. noun   **b.** verb

2. Which definition matches the meaning of *perfect* in this sentence?

   The audience clapped loudly because the performance was **perfect**.

   a. definition 1   **b.** definition 4

3. Which definition matches the meaning of *perfect* in this sentence?

   The new painting looked **perfect** above the sofa.

   a. definition 2   **b.** definition 3

4. How do you say *perfect* when it is a verb?

   a. **PER**-fect   **b.** per-**FECT**

ESSENTIAL QUESTION

How do I become who I want to be?

First Thoughts

1. What do you think the dance performance in the photo is about? Tell a partner.

2. What inspires someone to become a dancer? List two reasons. Use two words from the box in your response.

culture	encourage	knowledge	inspiration	interest	original	talented

_____

_____

Discuss How will you decide on your career? Rank these ideas in order from most important (1) to least important (6) for you. Then compare and discuss your rankings with a partner.

_____ You will earn a lot of money.   _____ The work will have a big impact on the world.

_____ You have a lot of interest in the work.   _____ The work is important to your culture.

_____ You have skills for this job.   _____ The job is what your family expects you to do.

Reading Skill: Analyze Events

Analyze the events in a nonfiction text to understand how they are connected and the impact they have on people or ideas in the text. To analyze events, follow these steps:

1. Determine the important events. An important event is one that causes change.

2. Identify the effect of the events. Ask yourself: *What happened because of this event? How did this event affect other people or ideas?*

3. Look for signal words that show cause and effect: *as a result, effect, because.*

Skill in Action

Read the text about Thomas Gallaudet and a reader's thoughts about the events. Complete the chart with the missing effects.

In the 1800s in the United States, people didn't send children who couldn't hear to school. They didn't think they could learn. But Thomas Gallaudet had a neighbor who was deaf. Gallaudet became her tutor. While he was teaching her, he noticed something important. If he explained ideas in writing, she understood. She was a talented learner. She just needed other ways to learn.

As a result, Gallaudet went to France to learn other ways to teach, and he discovered sign language. He learned these hand movements. After he returned to the U.S., he formed the first school for the deaf. It has given thousands of deaf children the chance to learn.

> Thomas tutored his deaf neighbor. As a result, he noticed deaf children could learn.

> He went to France to learn more about teaching. He discovered sign language there.

> After learning about sign language, Thomas opened a school in the United States for deaf children.

Event	Effect
Gallaudet tutored his deaf neighbor.	*He noticed deaf children could learn.*
Gallaudet went to France to learn more about teaching.	
Gallaudet opened the first school for deaf children.	

Amalia Hernández:
A Dancer's Dream

by **Jane Skinner**

Ballet Folklórico de México performing "Charreada"

"The future belongs to those who believe in the beauty of their dreams." — **Eleanor Roosevelt**

Amalia (ah-MAH-lee-ah) Hernández was born in Mexico City in 1917. Her family assumed she would **grow up** to be a schoolteacher like her mother and her grandmother. Even Ami (AH-me), as everyone called her, expected that.

Amalia Hernández

🎧 6.2

1   Amalia Hernández's dream was dance. Hernández was born in Mexico City on September 19th, 1917. Dance is an important part of Mexican **culture**. Traditional folk dances,[1] also called *danzas*, are loud, lively, and fun. While on a trip as a young girl, Hernández
5   saw danzas performed by dancers in bright costumes. It was very exciting! Right away, she knew she wanted to be a dancer, too.

However, Hernández's family expected her to **become** a teacher. Her mother had been a teacher. So had her grandmother. Hernández had other ideas for herself, though. She begged her
10   father for ballet lessons. It wasn't hard to convince him; her father wanted only the best for his daughter. He built a dance studio in their home. He hired one of the most **talented** ballet teachers to instruct her. Mr. and Mrs. Hernández **encouraged** their daughter in her lessons. Hernández practiced twirling, gliding, and leaping. She
15   stood on her toes and posed with arms out and head held high. She became an excellent ballerina. Over time, however, this creative, energetic girl knew she wanted to try a different kind of dance. She was ready to explore.

When Hernández was twenty-two years old, she watched
20   a special performance in Mexico City. Dancers from the United States had come to present an exciting new kind of dance called "modern dance." Modern dance combines ballet, folk dance, and social dance—a type of dance which often invites others to join in. It was different from anything she had seen before. The rules for
25   modern dance are less strict than for ballet. The **original**, free-flowing movements seem to come from the dancers' emotions.

STOP & THINK
Contrast
How is modern dance different from ballet?

---
[1] **folk dances** dances performed by common people in a country and often taught to children

Party in Tlacotalpan, influenced by the dances of Andalusia with African influences.

Hernández was inspired. Though she continued to practice ballet, she began taking modern dance lessons, too. She loved how it felt to express her feelings through movement set to music.

30   Hernández became as skilled at modern dance as she was at ballet. She performed as a dancer and loved her time on stage. In her twenties and early thirties, she also worked as a dance teacher with the Fine Arts National Institute in Mexico City. It was here she realized that while she enjoyed teaching, she also wanted

35   to become a choreographer. A choreographer is someone who creates his or her own dances. Hernández's dances would reflect her own visions[2] and not someone else's.

Ballet and modern dance, the forms Hernández had learned so well, have their own cultural backgrounds. Ballet began in Italy.

40   Modern dance began in the United States. Hernández loved both styles of dance. Yet she felt a strong desire to create something that represented Mexico. She thought back on the lively danzas that she had seen when she was a girl. Now, as a woman, she **decided** to choreograph dances that reflected her native country and its history.

45   In 1952, Hernández **formed** her own dance company[3] with eight dancers. The company was called the Ballet Folklórico de

> **STOP & THINK**
> **Infer** How can dance show culture?

---

[2] **visions** something you imagine; pictures you see in your mind
[3] **company** group of actors, dancers, or singers who perform together

México. Hernández traveled to towns and small villages all across Mexico to research traditional dances. She watched as dancers performed colorful danzas. Some of the dances were celebrations
50 to meet new friends. Others were ceremonies to bring a good harvest.[4] The dancers swirled and stomped in the sunlight. Hernández paid close attention to the rhythms, the music, the movements, and the clothes the dancers wore. She felt a close connection to the dances. Sometimes, she even joined in.

55 It was Hernández's goal, her dream, to create original dances and bring them to the stage. The **knowledge** she gained from her trips around the country helped her design dances similar to the bright, upbeat danzas. She also studied the ancient Aztec and Mayan people of Mexico, their culture, their art, and their
60 sculptures. Then she created pounding, rhythmic dances to reflect

> **STOP & THINK**
> **Recognize** What knowledge did Hernández use to create her dances? What made them original?

---

[4] **harvest** the amount of crops (corn, beans, etc.) gathered

◄ Crown of Montezuma (wool & feathers), Aztec

"The Dance of the Feather" is inspired by the Zapotec Indians and expresses welcome.

Amalia Hernández: A Dancer's Dream **223**

the power and strength of those early civilizations.[5] Not only did Hernández choreograph the dances, but she also had elaborate, flowing costumes made for her dancers. She used eye-catching sets and dramatic lighting for the stage. The dancers practiced hard to perfect the moves. Finally, they were ready.

In the early 1950's, the Ballet Folklórico de México gave their first performances. They were a unique combination of ballet, modern dance, and the danzas. They expressed the energy, beauty, and culture of Mexico. And they were a hit! People crowded the theater to watch. They were thrilled and moved by the spectacle.[6] The company quickly became famous. New dancers joined. Over the years, the number of dancers increased from eight to several hundred. In 1954, the company was invited to perform on television. The show was so popular that the dances became part of the weekly broadcast.

The Ballet Folklórico de México was invited to travel to countries around the world to share their unique and beautiful dances. At this point, Hernández stopped dancing herself so she could focus on directing, choreographing, and arranging travel. The company toured North America, Europe, Australia, and Japan. They won many awards and represented Mexico in the Pan American Games in Chicago in 1959.

In 1968, Hernández's company opened a dance school in Mexico City. She wanted to give young people the chance to discover an **interest** in dance. Students were taught modern dance, ballet, and Mexican folk dances. The school is still teaching dancers after all these years.

Amalia Hernández died in 2000. Yet her Ballet Folklórico de México is as vibrant as ever. The company continues to perform at the Palace of Fine Arts in Mexico City. It still travels the globe to offer her creative vision to the world. Hernández's dream of sharing her love of Mexico, its history, and its people with the world had become a reality.

> **STOP & THINK**
> **Analyze Events** What were the events that caused Hernández to stop dancing?

---

[5] **civilizations** well-developed and organized societies (people living together)
[6] **spectacle** very impressive show

Palacio de Bellas Artes
(Palace of Fine Arts),
Mexico City

Close Read

Work with a partner.

1. Determine the meanings of your underlined words and phrases.

2. Discuss the questions:

   What did Amalia Hernández become? Why?

Understand

Read the summary. Three sentences have errors. Rewrite the sentences and correct the errors.

> Hernández's mother and father encouraged her interest in dance. Hernández was a choreographer, and then she became a dancer. In 1952, she became a dance teacher. Hernández created dances from her knowledge of the cultures, people, and history of Mexico. The Ballet Folklórico de México became very successful and toured the world. In the end, Hernández opened a school because her family expected her to be a teacher.

1. _____

2. _____

3. _____

Apply the Skill: Analyze Events

Analyze these events in the story. Write the effect of each event in the chart. Then discuss your ideas with a partner.

Event	Effect
As a young girl, Hernández sees dancers while on a trip.	
Hernández decided that she wanted to create dances to reflect Mexico and its history.	
The company becomes famous and tours the world.	

Read Again and Analyze

Read the text again and respond to the questions. Use evidence from the text to support your responses.

1. **Focus** How did Hernández become such a good dancer?

2. **Explain** Why did Hernández decide to be a choreographer and form a dance company?

3. **Identify** What were four different inspirations for Hernández's dances?

4. **Examine** Name three important decisions Hernández made in her life.

5. **Infer** Why is the Ballet Folklórico de México still popular today?

Share Your Perspective

Discuss the questions in a small group.

1. What type of person was Amalia Hernández? What advice do you think she would give to young people?

2. How important is it to have someone encourage you in your career path and life decisions? Do you think Hernández's life would have been different if her parents hadn't encouraged her dream? Why or why not?

3. Do you know people who have achieved their dreams? What did they become? How did they do it?

Discussion Frames

In my opinion, Amalia Hernández was …

She would say …

From my perspective, it's very important to …

Reflect

How does "Amalia Hernández: A Dancer's Dream" help you understand how people become who they want to be? With a partner, use some of the words to write sentences about the text.

Nouns	Verbs	Adjectives
culture inspiration interest knowledge	become decide encourage expect form grow up	original talented

_____

_____

_____

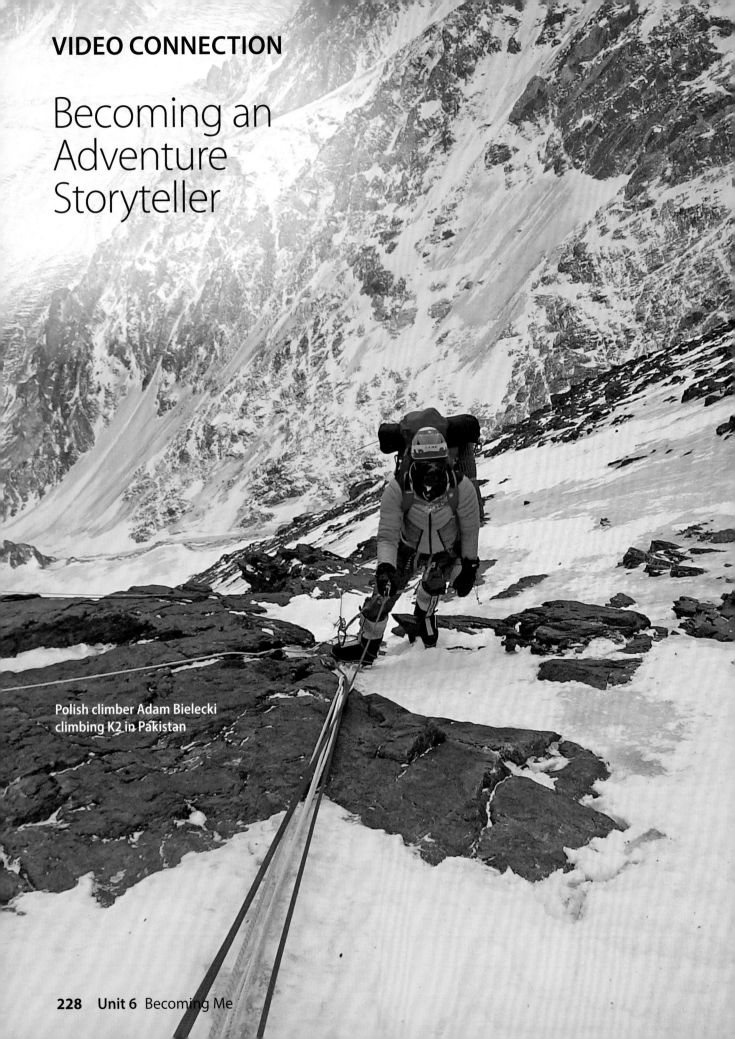

Becoming an Adventure Storyteller

Polish climber Adam Bielecki climbing K2 in Pakistan

First Thoughts

Look at the photo. If you were going to climb this mountain, what song would you listen to before you did it? Why? Share ideas with a partner.

Viewing Skill: Identify Mood

When you watch a video, consider how the music, visuals, and speaker's tone of voice help you identify the mood. How do the images and music make you feel? What feelings does the speaker's tone of voice show?

Apply the Skill

▶ **6.1** Watch each part of the video. Write short descriptions in the chart. Use the first three columns to help you identify the mood.

	Images	Music	Speaker's Voice	Mood
Part 1				
Part 2				
Part 3				

Understand and Analyze

▶ **6.2** Watch the video. Answer the questions. Support your responses with evidence from the video.

1. **Restate** What interests did Fitz Cahall have as a boy?
2. **Recognize** Cahall almost gave up on his dream. Why did he decide not to?
3. **Infer** What is an adventure storyteller? Who are the Adventurers of the Year?
4. **Examine** How does Cahall feel about his life's decisions?

Share Your Perspective

Discuss the questions in a small group.

1. How much of what you achieve in life is based on talent? How much is based on determination?
2. What does it mean to "live on your own terms"? What are your terms?

> **Discussion Frames**
>
> I think that __% is based on talent because …
>
> To "live on your own terms" means to …

Reflect on the Essential Question

Think about how the characters and people in this unit become who they want to be. Write your ideas in the idea web.

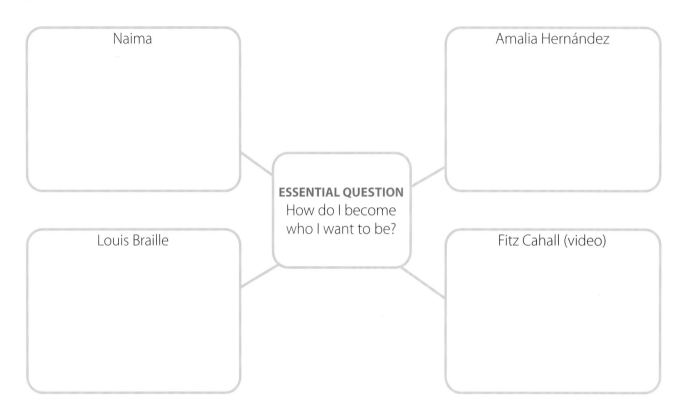

Naima

Amalia Hernández

ESSENTIAL QUESTION
How do I become
who I want to be?

Louis Braille

Fitz Cahall (video)

Discuss the Essential Question

Look at your ideas about the Essential Question earlier in the unit and your notes in the idea web above. How have your ideas about the Essential Question changed? What changed your ideas? Discuss your answers in a group.

Respond to the Essential Question

Write your response to the Essential Question.

Response Rubric
A good response will
✓ state your opinion
✓ provide support from the texts, the discussion, and your life
✓ use theme vocabulary

Theme Vocabulary

become (v.)
decide (v.)
grow up (v. phr.)
inspiration (n.)
interest (n.)
talented (adj.)

Option 1: Make a Short Training Video

What can your class learn from you? Make a short training video to share your skills or talent. Explain how to do something, such as cook a favorite recipe, do a skateboard trick, or play a musical instrument.

Example:

Hi, I'm Kiara and <u>I'm going to show you how to</u> draw a portrait. <u>First, you will need</u> a pencil and a notebook for sketching. <u>Second, you will need</u> someone you can draw. <u>It's best to</u> draw a friend or family member who can sit still for you. Have the person sit about two feet away from you. <u>Then</u> draw the outline of his or her face. <u>Remember to</u> look at the person while you sketch. A mistake many people make is looking at their drawing instead of the person. <u>You need to</u> draw what you see, not what you think the person looks like …

1. Write your video script. Look at the example. Use the underlined phrases to help you write your script.

2. Make your video.

3. Post the video to a class website.

4. Watch a classmate's video and try it out. Leave a comment for your classmate. Let them know how it went. You can say, "I tried to … and it was really fun because …" or "You gave great directions for …"

Option 2: Create an Artwork

Create a song, dance, painting, poem, or other work of art that shows your culture.

A common type of alpana called *Rangoli* outside a home in Hyderabad, India ▼

1. Learn more about the alpanas from *Rickshaw Girl*. Why do people create them? Then think about Amalia Hernández's dances. How do they show her culture?

2. Now think about your own culture. What is important to it? Make a list of your ideas.

3. Create an original artwork to show some of your ideas.

4. Present your work of art and ideas to a small group.

Assignment: Write a Biography

A **biography** is the true story of a person's life, written by another person. In this assignment, you will write a short biography (2 paragraphs) of a person who inspires you. Your biography will include the following:

- a title that describes something important about the person
- events from the person's life in the order in which they happened
- a paragraph that describes the person's early life, including his or her interests or inspirations
- a paragraph that describes how the person became who he or she wanted to be
- a sentence that states the impact the person had on the world

Explore the Model

Read the model. Look at the events the writer included. What phrases help you understand the order of events?

Language for Writing

Read the model again.

1. Underline additional sentences that show Goddard's interests or inspirations.

2. Find one possessive noun and one possessive adjective. Write them in the chart.

Possessive Noun	Possessive Adjective

3. The writer uses words and phrases to show cause and effect. Complete the sentences with the words from the model. Notice when a comma is used.

As a young boy, he was often sick, _____ his mom kept him home from school.

_____ , he spent a lot of his time reading.

Dr. Robert H. Goddard posing next to his liquid-fueled rocket

Rocket Man

Biographies give dates that show the order of events in a person's life.

The first paragraph describes Goddard's early life. One of his interests was reading books about space.

The second paragraph describes how Goddard became who he wanted to be.

The concluding sentence states the impact Goddard had on the world.

In 1882, Robert Goddard was born in Massachusetts in the United States. As a young boy, he was often sick, so his mom kept him home from school. As a result, he spent a lot of his time reading. He loved books about space. He dreamed of making a machine to fly into space. On October 19, 1899, he climbed a tree and looked up at the sky. He imagined going to Mars. After that moment, he knew what he wanted to do with his life. He never forgot that day.

He studied space in college and continued to think about traveling to Mars. He asked important questions. How fast can human bodies travel? What can carry them into space? And how can they get there? He experimented with his ideas. On March 16, 1926, he became the first person to successfully launch a rocket powered by liquid fuel toward the sky. He continued to search for ways to reach space. He died in 1945, but Goddard's ideas did not. They are the reasons we've touched the moon and flown into space.

Plan Your Writing

Complete the outline.

- Choose a person who inspires you.
- Write information about the person in the outline.
- Include details about the person's interests or inspirations and important events in his or her life.
- Describe his or her impact on the world.
- Include a title that describes something important about the person.

Outline

Title:
Early Life:
Name of person:
Year and place of birth:
Early interests or inspirations:
Later Life:
Event:
Event:
Impact on the world:

Write and Revise

Write Use your outline to write a first draft.

- Include specific dates so the reader can follow the order of events.
- Use words to show cause and effect.

Revise Exchange biographies with a partner. Using the checklist, review your partner's work and give feedback. Use feedback from your partner to revise your draft.

☐ Does the writer include phrases and dates to show the order of events in the person's life?

☐ Does the first paragraph explain the person's early life, including his or her interests or inspirations?

☐ Does the second paragraph explain how the person became who he or she wanted to be?

☐ Does the writer state the impact the person had on the world?

Proofread Check the grammar, spelling, punctuation, and capitalization in your biography. Make edits to correct any errors.

TIP

Check that you've used possessive nouns and adjectives correctly. Circle possessive nouns and underline possessive adjectives.

Publish

Share your biography. Read two of your classmates' biographies.

Present Your Biography

You will give a short speech on the person you wrote about. You will share a picture of the person, discuss his or her early life, and tell about the person's impact on the world.

Prepare your speech:

- Underline important events from the person's early life in the biography.
- Circle important events that show who the person became and his or her impact on the world.
- Practice reading the important events from your biography. Share your speech with a partner.

Share your speech in a small group.

- Listen to your classmates' speeches, and write an interesting detail about each one. What makes the person original?
- Make a note of any questions you have and ask them at the end of each speech.

TAKE ACTION

Brendan Mullan speaking at National Geographic headquarters in Washington, D. C.

Inspiring Young Astronomers ∩ 6.3

EXPLORER IN ACTION
Brendan Mullan is an astronomer and educator.

Brendan Mullan wants to share his knowledge with others so they, too, can discover the wonders of space. In his words, "Human beings fundamentally want to connect with some cosmic context greater than themselves. I want to give them that chance."

Mullan's interest in space started with a trip to the planetarium[1] when he was young. His passion led him to study astronomy and become a researcher and teacher at Pennsylvania State University. Mullan works with middle school students in summer camp, too. Students do experiments to look for life on other planets and to hunt for planets around other stars. He became an educator to inspire others. He states, "What could be more fun and meaningful than sharing the majesty of the cosmos with everyone?"

---

1 **planetarium** building that shows the stars and planets in the night sky

▶ 6.3 Answer the questions. Then watch the video to learn more.

1. Brendan grew up and became a _____ because he wanted to _____.

2. Brendan became interested in space because _____

_____

How Will You Take Action?

Choose one or more of these actions to do.

Personal

Create a vision board of your future.

1. Visualizing the future is a way to achieve it.
2. Cut out pictures and words that show your goals for the future. You can use magazines or print words and pictures found online.
3. Post your pictures and words on a posterboard to hang in your room. Reflect on your goals each week. Continue to add photos and words that inspire you!

School

Join or create a mentor program in your school.

1. A mentor is an experienced person who gives help, advice, or training. How can your school connect students with mentors? (Consider the readings. Who were mentors for Naima and Amalia Hernández?)
2. Discuss ideas for mentors in small groups, and create a plan so students can get the knowledge and encouragement they need to succeed.

Local

Interview a person from your community who inspires you.

1. Write three questions to ask the person about his or her life.
2. Ask your questions and record the interview. Write a short summary.
3. Post the summaries online to share the inspiring stories with your community.

Global

Do a cultural exchange with another school.

1. Invite students from another school to teach about their culture and teach them about yours.
2. Work in small groups. Create a presentation to discuss one aspect of culture (food, festivals, language, art, etc.). Record your presentation.
3. Share the videos with the other school, and enjoy learning about their culture.

Reflect

Reflect on your Take Action project(s). Then complete the sentences.

1. My project(s) was/were successful because _____
   _____.

2. One thing I wish I had done differently is _____
   _____.

3. Because of what I learned in this unit, one thing I will do is _____
   _____.

"I took a walk in the woods and came out taller than the trees."
—**HENRY DAVID THOREAU, AMERICAN NATURALIST**

What does this quote mean to you?

Look at the photo and caption. Discuss the questions.

1. Describe the animal. How does looking at it make you feel?

2. Why might this caterpillar make itself look like a snake?

◄ **A spicebush swallowtail caterpillar making itself look like a snake, Washington, D.C.**

ESSENTIAL QUESTION
How does nature affect us?

Theme Vocabulary

Use these words to express your ideas throughout the unit.

PRACTICE 1 Read the conversation. Think about the meaning of each word in **bold**. Then write each word next to its definition in the chart below.

> Why do you think people spend time in nature?

> I think people want to feel less **stress**. They take a break from their busy lives. For example, I love hiking. In the woods, there's **peace** and quiet. I feel calm.

> I agree. It's good for our **mental health**. At school, we can sit outside at lunch. I think it helps **reduce** my stress. I forget about my homework and just enjoy the sun. After that, I can **concentrate** in class. It's easier to pay attention.

Theme Vocabulary

concentrate (v.)
health (n.)
mental (adj.)
peace (n.)
reduce (v.)
stress (n.)

Word	Definition
health	being well, not sick
	relating to the mind (thinking)
	a quiet, calm state
	to focus one's attention on something
	a state of worry caused by problems in one's life
	to make something smaller in size, amount, or number

PRACTICE 2 Work with a partner. Answer the questions about the conversation.

1. What does the conversation suggest is a cause of stress?

2. What do the students do to reduce stress?

3. How does nature affect the students' mental health?

Explore the Essential Question

Think How important is nature to you? For each question below, choose the answer that best describes you.

1. You have 30 minutes of free time. How do you want to spend it?

    a. outside, sitting in a park or walking by the water

    b. on a screen, talking with friends or playing a video game

2. Which kind of photo do you want for the wallpaper image on your phone?

    a. a nature scene (waterfall, mountains, sunset)

    b. a picture of your friends or family

3. Where do you want to work in the future?

    a. outside in a natural area, in a forest, or on a farm

    b. at a hospital, a university, or an office

4. You decide to join a volunteer group. Which one do you choose?

    a. a group that plants flowers and trees in your city

    b. a group that provides technology to people who need it

5. You are planning a vacation. Where do you want to go?

    a. the mountains or the beach

    b. museums, restaurants, and the theater

Discuss With a partner, discuss your answers above. Explain your reasons.

Respond Circle the words related to nature. Add your own ideas. Then use some of the words to complete the sentences below. Share your ideas with a partner.

peace animals **gardens**

ocean food

stress **health** **nature** air **break** **exercise**

mountains parks

calm

inspiring **plants** **beautiful**

I like to visit _____ because _____.

Nature is important because _____.

Key Vocabulary

PRACTICE Look at the photos and read the sentences. Discuss the meaning of the words in **bold** with a partner. Then ask and answer the questions.

despair (noun)
The sad news brought him much **despair**.
When someone feels despair, what can you say or do?

lonely (adjective)
It can feel **lonely** to be by yourself.
What do you do when you feel lonely?

mood (noun)
She's always in a good **mood** during gym class.
When are you in a good mood?

pleasure (noun)
He enjoys cooking. It gives him a lot of **pleasure**.
What activity gives you pleasure?

wander (verb)
It's nice to **wander** along the beach and look out at the water.
Where do you like to wander?

wild (adjective)
Be quiet. Don't scare the **wild** animals.
What wild animals have you seen?

Vocabulary: Analyze Word Choice

Poets choose their words carefully to have an effect on the reader. Follow these steps to analyze word choice:

1. Read the title and the poem to understand its main idea.

2. Then read each line again. Notice the nouns, adjectives, and verbs. Ask yourself: *Why did the poet choose these words? What do they help me see and feel?*

3. As you read each line, notice if the descriptions are similar to or different from those in the line before it. What ideas is the poet discussing? Do the words create positive or negative feelings?

The word *peace* makes me feel calm.

Despair is very different from *peace*. When you have despair, you don't have hope.

Example:

The Peace of Wild Things

1 When despair for the world grows in me
2 and I wake in the night at the least sound
3 in fear of what my life and my children's lives may be,
4 I go and lie down where the wood drake
5 rests in his beauty on the water, and the great heron feeds.

A feeling grows on its own. You can't control it. I think the poet chose this verb because it doesn't feel good to have despair growing.

This word is negative.

PRACTICE 1 Do the words in each line of the poem above create positive or negative feelings? For each line, list the important words. Then write *positive* or *negative*.

Line 1 *despair, grows (negative)*

Line 2 _____

Line 3 _____

Line 4 _____

Line 5 _____

PRACTICE 2 What other words and phrases could a poet use to describe despair and peace? Discuss with a partner, and add your ideas to the chart.

Despair	Peace

ESSENTIAL QUESTION

How does nature affect us?

First Thoughts

1. What do you see in the photo? Tell a partner.

2. How does the photo make you feel?

_____

_____

3. Write a title for a possible poem about this photo. _____

Discuss Check (✔) the statements that are true for you. Then discuss your answers with a group.

☐ I find peace in pictures of nature. I enjoy looking at the beauty of nature.

☐ I like to watch wild animals on nature shows, at the park, or at the zoo.

☐ I can name many animals and plants in the natural world.

☐ I can remember a time when I was in nature, and I like to think about it.

☐ I am in a good mood when I'm in nature. It gives me pleasure to be outside.

☐ I want to spend more time in nature.

Reading Skill: Analyze the Text Structure of a Poem

Poems have a different **text structure**, or form, than stories and articles. Analyze the text structure of a poem to help you understand its meaning. As you read a poem, think about the following:

1. Poets group words into lines. Pause after reading each line, and think about the idea it's communicating. Also, notice any lines that are repeated. These ideas are important.

2. Poets group lines into stanzas, like writers put sentences into paragraphs. What does each stanza describe? How do ideas change from one stanza to the next?

3. Poets often write poems to be read aloud. Read the poem aloud, and listen for words that rhyme at the end of each line, such as *cloud* and *crowd*. Notice the pattern.

Skill in Action

Read aloud the stanzas from "I Wandered Lonely as a Cloud." Look at the reader's thoughts. With a partner, discuss the following:

1. What image does each stanza describe?

2. What pairs of rhyming words does the poet use at the ends of the lines?

> The title is the same as the first line. Feeling lonely is an important idea in this poem.

I Wandered Lonely as a Cloud

> The first stanza uses six lines. They describe the poet's feelings and what he saw.

1. I wandered lonely as a cloud
2. That floats on high o'er vales and hills,
3. When all at once I saw a crowd,
4. A host, of golden daffodils;
5. Beside the lake, beneath the trees,
6. Fluttering and dancing in the breeze.

> The words at the end of the lines rhyme. The rhyming words are important.

> This stanza also uses six lines. But in this stanza, the feeling of being lonely is gone.

7. Continuous as the stars that shine
8. And twinkle on the milky way,
9. They stretched in never-ending line
10. Along the margin of a bay:
11. Ten thousand saw I at a glance,
12. Tossing their heads in sprightly dance.

The Peace of Wild Things

by **Wendell Berry**

A heron flying low over water, Pantanal region, Brazil

1   When **despair** for the world grows in me

and I wake in the night at the least sound

in fear of what my life and my children's lives may be,

I go and lie down where the wood drake

5   rests in his beauty on the water, and the great heron feeds.

I come into the **peace** of **wild** things

who do not tax[1] their lives with forethought[2]

of grief. I come into the presence of still water.

And I feel above me the day-blind stars

10   waiting with their light. For a time

I rest in the grace[3] of the world, and am free.

---

[1] **tax** to burden or make more difficult
[2] **forethought** thinking ahead of time
[3] **grace** beauty

STOP & THINK
Examine How does the poet describe the stars? Is it day or night in the poem?

**About the Poet
(b. 1934)**

Wendell Berry is a poet and writer of fiction and nonfiction essays. He has lived on a farm in Kentucky in the United States for more than forty years. He believes that there is nothing more important than our relationship with nature.

I Wandered Lonely as a Cloud

by **William Wordsworth**

About the Poet
(1770–1850)

William Wordsworth is one of the most famous English poets. He wrote during the Industrial Revolution. As people moved to cities and created factories and machines, Wordsworth wrote about the value of nature.

Daffodils growing in a field at sunset, Vancouver Island, British Columbia, Canada

1   I **wandered lonely** as a cloud
    That floats on high o'er vales[1] and hills,
    When all at once I saw a crowd,
    A host, of golden daffodils;
5   Beside the lake, beneath the trees,
    Fluttering and dancing in the breeze.

    Continuous as the stars that shine
    And twinkle on the milky way,
    They stretched in never-ending line
10 Along the margin of a bay:
    Ten thousand saw I at a glance,
    Tossing their heads in sprightly[2] dance.

    The waves beside them danced; but they
    Out-did the sparkling waves in glee[3]:
15 A poet could not but be gay,[4]
    In such a jocund[5] company:
    I gazed—and gazed—but little thought
    What wealth the show to me had brought:

    For oft, when on my couch I lie
20 In vacant or in pensive[6] **mood**,
    They flash upon that inward eye
    Which is the bliss[7] of solitude[8];
    And then my heart with **pleasure** fills,
    And dances with the daffodils.

> **STOP & THINK**
> **Analyze Word Choice** What words does Wordsworth use to describe the daffodils? What feelings do the words show?

---

[1] **vales** valleys
[2] **sprightly** full of life
[3] **glee** happiness
[4] **gay (not used often today)** happy
[5] **jocund (not used often today)** happy
[6] **pensive** thoughtful
[7] **bliss** happiness
[8] **solitude** being alone

Close Read

Work with a partner.

1. Determine the meanings of your underlined words and phrases.
2. Discuss the question:

   What story does each poem tell?

Apply the Skill: Analyze the Text Structure of a Poem

Write answers to the questions for each poem.

Questions	The Peace of Wild Things	I Wandered Lonely as a Cloud
1. How many stanzas are in the poem?		
2. How many lines are in a stanza?		
3. Is there a rhyme pattern?		
4. Does the poet repeat words?		
5. Does each line begin with a capital letter?		

Understand

Read the statements, and check (✔) the correct answer for Poem 1 ("The Peace of Wild Things"), Poem 2 ("I Wandered Lonely as a Cloud"), or both poems.

	Poem 1	Poem 2	Both
1. In the poem, wild animals bring feelings of peace.	☐	☐	☐
2. In the poem, nature's beauty brings happiness.	☐	☐	☐
3. The poem contrasts feelings of calm with fear.	☐	☐	☐
4. The poem contrasts feeling alone with feeling pleasure.	☐	☐	☐
5. The poem names wild things in the natural world.	☐	☐	☐
6. In the poem, being in nature improves mental health.	☐	☐	☐

Read Again and Analyze

Read the poems again and respond to the questions. Use evidence from the text to support your responses.

1. **Recognize** What does the poet in "The Peace of Wild Things" feel stressed or worried about?

2. **Summarize** What does the poet in "The Peace of Wild Things" do to improve his mood? Why?

3. **Relate** What does it mean to wander "lonely as a cloud"? How do the other descriptions of nature in this poem help you understand the poet's feelings?

4. **Distinguish** Which stanzas of "I Wandered Lonely as a Cloud" describe the past? Which stanza describes the present moment in the poem?

5. **Illustrate** How are the poems similar? Give two examples from each poem to show how they are alike.

Share Your Perspective

Discuss the questions in a small group.

1. What are your favorite lines from the poems? Why?

2. Think of another title for each poem. Which title do you like best? Why?

3. How is reading the lines of a poem different from reading text in paragraphs? Do you like to read poetry? Why or why not?

Discussion Frames

My favorite lines are … because …

Another title could be …

Reading a poem is different because …

Reflect

How do "The Peace of Wild Things" and "I Wandered Lonely as a Cloud" help you understand how nature affects us? With a partner, use some of the words to write sentences about the poems.

Nouns	Verbs	Adjectives
despair health mood peace pleasure stress	concentrate reduce wander	lonely mental wild

_____

_____

_____

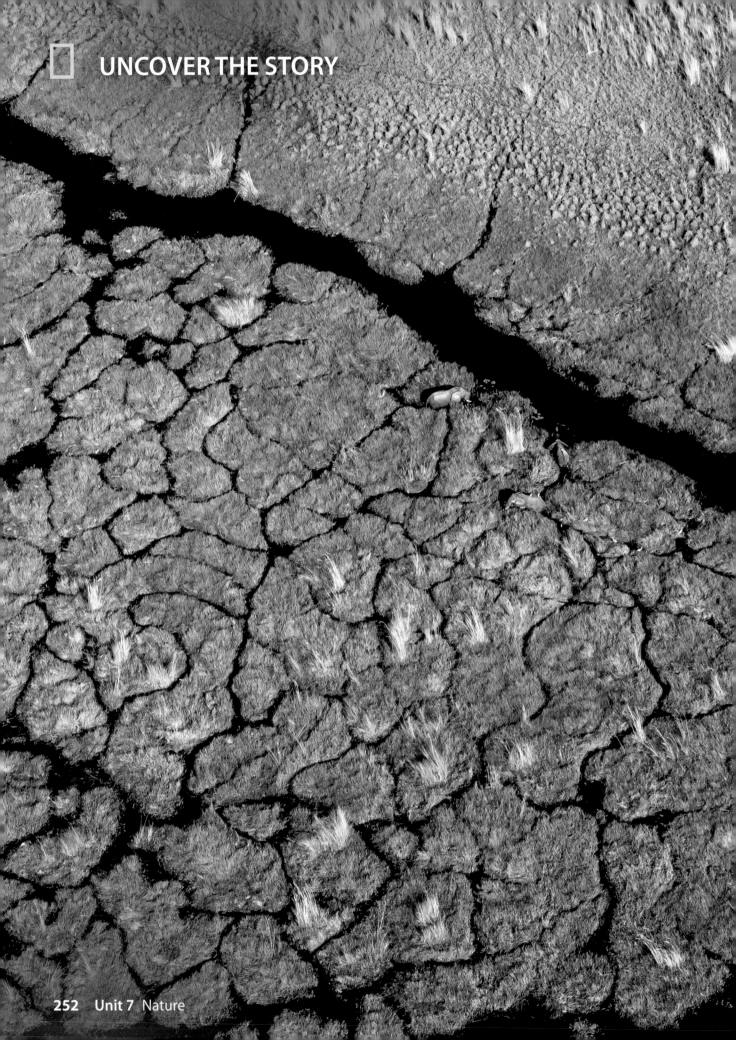

Examine the Photo

1. Look at the photo. What do you see?

2. How do you think this photo relates to nature and how it affects us?

3. Write 3–5 questions about the photo. Discuss them with a small group.

Find Out ▶ 7.1

Watch photographer Beverly Joubert talk about her photo.

1. Did she answer any of your questions? Which ones?

2. Why does Joubert call elephants the "landscape architects" or "gardeners" of the Okavango?

3. What effect do the elephants have on other animals? On people in the local communities?

Reflect

Beverly Joubert takes photos of wildlife. How do you think this lifestyle has affected her? How would it make you feel?

Share Your Story

Share a photo in a group.

1. Take or find a photo of an animal that you know about or want to learn more about.

2. Find information about the animal and other animals it interacts with. What are some positive (or negative) ways it affects these animals?

3. Share the photo and information about the animal with a group.

ABOUT THE PHOTOGRAPHER

Beverly Joubert is a conservationist and filmmaker. She helps save wildlife and preserve natural habitats.

Key Vocabulary

PRACTICE Look at the photos and read the sentences. Discuss the meaning of the words in **bold** with a partner. Then ask and answer the questions.

anxious (adjective)
She felt **anxious** about the important test.
How do you help someone who is feeling anxious?

benefit (noun)
A **benefit** of working in a small group is learning from others.
Do you like working in a small group or with the whole class? What are the benefits of each?

disease (noun)
A **disease** made the plant sick.
What diseases affect people?

physical (adjective)
A doctor checks your **physical** health.
What are signs of good physical health?

research (noun)
Scientists do **research** to learn more about the brain.
What other kinds of research should we do?

protect (verb)
A helmet **protects** your head if you fall.
What parts of her body is this skater protecting?

Grammar: Compound and Complex Sentences

Compound Sentences

We link two independent clauses (sentences) to form a **compound sentence**. Use a coordinating conjunction (such as *and, or, but, so, yet,* or *nor*) to link the clauses.

Place a comma before the coordinating conjunction.

The city has a beautiful park, and there are many paths for walking and biking.

Complex Sentences

We form a **complex sentence** by linking an independent clause with a dependent clause. A dependent clause begins with a subordinating conjunction (such as *when, because, if,* or *after*). A dependent clause can come before or after the independent clause. If the dependent clause comes first, then use a comma after it.

If people spend more time outside, they are more likely to get exercise.
I always feel better after I exercise.

PRACTICE 1 Read each sentence. Circle the conjunction. Underline each independent clause. Then write *compound* or *complex*.

1. High-school students remember more content from school (when) they learn it outside. ___*complex*___

2. After school, most students do homework, or sometimes they play sports. _____

3. After people spend time in nature, they feel less stressed. _____

4. Kids need time to study, but they also need time for outdoor activities. _____

5. Exercise is important because it improves our health. _____

PRACTICE 2 Combine the sentences, using the conjunction in parentheses. Add commas where necessary.

1. You can't concentrate. It's difficult to learn. (if)

   _____

2. People could walk more. They could go for a run. (or)

   _____

3. There are not many parks in my city. I live close to one. (but)

   _____

4. I look at pictures of nature. I feel less anxious. (after)

   _____

5. Scientists are studying the causes of heart disease. They are looking at ways to treat it. (and)

   _____

ESSENTIAL QUESTION

How does nature affect us?

First Thoughts

1. Look only at one of the two photos (Photo 1 or Photo 2) for one minute. Then respond to the questions below.

Photo 1

Photo 2

2. Which words best describe how you feel after looking at the photo? What effect does this photo have on you?

3. Imagine you have a 20-minute break. Which view would you want to look at? Why? What effect do you think it will have on you? Tell a partner.

Discuss Answer the questions. Then discuss your answers in a small group.

Questions	Answers
How much time do you spend in nature each week?	
How many times a day do you see a picture of nature or a nature scene, such as trees or plants?	
Where do you like to walk or do other physical activity?	
How often during the school day is it hard for you to concentrate?	
What do you do to feel better when you feel anxious?	

Reading Skill: Identify Claims in an Argument

In **argumentative** writing, the author shares his or her point of view on a topic. The argument includes claims and evidence. A **claim** is a statement that the author believes is true. To convince the reader of a point of view, the author supports the claim with evidence. To identify claims in an argument, follow these steps:

1. Identify the author's point of view on the topic. For example, ask, "What does the author think about nature?" Sentences that express the author's point of view are the claims.

2. Identify the evidence the author uses to support each claim. The author may use facts, statistics, examples, reasons, and expert opinions.

   - A fact is true information, such as "In France, all new business buildings must have a 'green roof.'"

   - A statistic is a type of fact that uses numbers or percentages, such as "In forest schools, kids can spend up to 95 percent of their school day outside in nature."

Skill in Action

Read the paragraph from "Why We Need Nature" and a reader's thoughts. What is the claim, and what is the evidence in this paragraph? Then discuss with a partner. Underline the claim.

The author's view is that nature is good for our mental health.

A forest bath is an example of connecting with nature.

This research shows facts. People have fewer stress hormones after they are in nature.

To start, connecting with nature is good for our mental health. Yoshifumi Miyazaki is an environmental science professor. He has written many books about the healing power of nature. He says, "When we are surrounded by nature, a feeling of comfort comes over us and our bodies relax." The forest baths of Japan have proven him right. A forest bath doesn't require a bathtub. You just unplug from your devices, go outside, and enjoy nature. You can simply lie in the grass, or you can walk through a park. Do forest baths work? Scientists say yes! For their research, they collected saliva[1] from people before and after a forest bath. They found lower amounts of stress hormones[2] in the saliva after people spent time in nature. In other words, nature reduces stress. Less stress makes people feel happier and less anxious.

Miyazaki is an expert. The author shares his opinion. It supports the idea that nature is good for our mental health.

Here is a reason that nature is good for our mental health.

[1] **saliva** the liquid in the mouth that helps break down food
[2] **hormones** substances made in the body that affect health

Read and answer the question: **What action does the author want the reader to take?** As you read, underline any parts of the text you have questions about or find confusing.

Why We Need Nature

by **Katie Parker**

🎧 7.3

1   Our planet has so many beautiful places to explore. There are city parks and wooded forests. There is rolling farmland and snowy mountains. So, why aren't we going outside? Now, more than ever, people are spending time indoors. We are working more
5   and spending more time on electronic devices.[1] We have more homework, too. It's true we are getting more done, but at what cost? About 28–32 percent of teens in the UAE described themselves as **anxious** in 2020. It's not much different in other countries. Still, some are rediscovering the **benefits** of the outdoors. In Japan,
10   doctors treat their patients with healing "forest baths." In Nordic countries, young children in forest schools spend most of their days outside. The rest of the world is studying ideas like these and finding that we need nature. It's becoming clear that spending time in nature can lead to a healthier future for us and for the planet.

15   To start, connecting with nature is good for our **mental health**. Yoshifumi Miyazaki is an environmental science professor. He has written many books about the healing power of nature. He says, "When we are surrounded by nature, a feeling of comfort comes over us and our bodies relax." The forest baths of Japan have proven him right.

[1] **electronic devices** objects such as phones or tablets

"*In every walk with Nature one receives far more than he seeks.*"

—*John Muir*

Bamboo forest in rural Japan

20 A forest bath doesn't require a bathtub. You just unplug from your devices, go outside, and enjoy nature. You can simply lie in the grass, or you can walk through a park. Do forest baths work? Scientists say yes! For their **research**, they collected saliva[2] from people before and after a forest bath. After people spent time in
25 nature, scientists found lower amounts of stress hormones[3] in the saliva. In other words, nature **reduces stress**. Less stress makes people feel happier and less anxious.

By allowing ourselves the gift of nature, we can improve our **physical** health, too. Nature reduces stress, which can lower blood
30 pressure and heart rate and loosen muscles. It makes the immune system[4] stronger. That means we're better **protected** from colds

> **STOP & THINK**
> **Explain** Explain the research study. What question did the scientists ask? How did they test it, and what did they learn?

Students of Samsø Frie Skole look through a magnifying glass during science class in Samsø, Denmark.

and viruses. Also, if people spend more time outside, they are more likely to get exercise. That's important, because exercise reduces the chances of getting **diseases** like diabetes and heart disease. It helps you build muscle and strong lungs. There are other physical benefits to spending time in nature. For example, in some countries in the Middle East and Southeast Asia, doctors noticed more and more children needing glasses. Scientists added 40 minutes of extra outside time to one group of students. These children developed fewer vision problems than other students.

We even learn better outside. In Nordic countries, "forest schools" are popular. Kids can spend up to 95 percent of their school day outside in nature. Compare that to other countries. In the U.S., some first-graders are in school 6–7 hours each day but have less than 20 minutes outdoors. In Taiwan, high school is a full day with almost no physical activity! You might think that school in the outdoors would lead to lower academic achievement, but you'd be wrong. Kids from Nordic countries have some of the highest academic marks and lowest stress in the world. Studies suggest that kids who spend time in "outdoor classrooms" *want* to learn more. They're more curious and confident. They can **concentrate** better. In one study, students were 54 percent less likely to lose focus after they had class *outside*. Learning outside helps students concentrate when they are *inside*. A 20-minute walk in the woods helped children with attention problems concentrate better. High-school students even remember more of what they've learned in school when they learn it outside.

To test the connection between nature and learning, a researcher named David Strayer took some volunteers on a camping trip. Before leaving, Strayer gave the volunteers some tasks. He used scans[5] to measure brain activity. After three days of camping, the volunteers performed 50 percent better on the tasks than before! Their brain activity confirmed that the volunteers were thinking more clearly. Science has proven that nature can improve focus, memory, and problem-solving. Not only do people FEEL better after time in nature, but we actually THINK better.

> **STOP & THINK**
> **Infer** How do you think the scientists learned that a 20-minute walk helped children concentrate? Describe the test.

---

[5] **scans** pictures of the inside of the body

The connection between humans and nature is very powerful. People far from nature can reduce stress levels and improve focus just by looking at pictures of greenery. Just looking at nature can improve learning and lower

70 stress. In another study, scientists gave students a brain break for 20 minutes. One break room had no windows. The second room had a view of an empty lot. The third room had a view of greenery. The students in the third room were the only students who were not distracted in

75 class afterward. The mental break allowed their brains to recover from being busy.

We are learning to value nature by spending time there—and that's a good thing, because we humans protect what we love. We have harmed nature by

80 polluting and destroying habitats.[6] Now, we are planting new gardens and trees to improve air quality. We are forming groups to protect local habitats. Globally, countries around the world have joined together to reduce pollution. In France, all new business buildings

85 must have a "green roof." These roofs are covered with plants that soak up pollution and provide bird and insect habitats. China is doing even more with green roofs. Liuzhou Forest City will be the first of its kind. Every building will have green roofs and walls. The city will

90 only use renewable energy,[7] and there will be many parks for forest bathing. We need to care for nature, so nature can care for us.

Whether you live in a city or the country, we need to rediscover nature, for both our health and the health of

95 our planet.

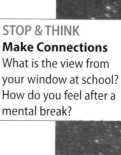

STOP & THINK
Make Connections
What is the view from your window at school? How do you feel after a mental break?

---

[6] **habitats** places where plants and animals live
[7] **renewable energy** power that can be replaced by nature (e.g., wind, solar)

Camping in the Rila mountains
beneath a sky full of stars, Bulgaria

Close Read

Work with a partner.

1. Determine the meanings of your underlined words and phrases.
2. Discuss the question:

   What action does the author want the reader to take?

Apply the Skill: Identify Claims in an Argument

Complete the missing information for the claims and evidence in the argument.

Claim 1: *By allowing ourselves the gift of nature, we can improve our physical health, too.*

Evidence:

1. *Nature reduces stress, and less stress lowers blood pressure and heart rate and loosens muscles.*
2. _____
   _____
3. _____
   _____

Claim 2: _____

Evidence:

1. *In Nordic countries, "forest schools" are popular. Kids from Nordic countries have some of the highest academic marks and lowest stress in the world.*
2. _____
   _____
3. _____

Understand

Choose the correct answers.

1. What is an example of a forest bath?
   - **a.** walking through nature
   - **b.** listening to wild animals
   - **c.** taking a bath to relax
2. What is a mental benefit of spending time in nature?
   - **a.** building strong muscles
   - **b.** feeling less stress
   - **c.** getting more exercise
3. What is a physical benefit of spending time in nature?
   - **a.** higher stress hormones
   - **b.** fewer vision problems
   - **c.** more forest schools
4. Which shows a result from a research study?
   - **a.** lower stress hormones in saliva
   - **b.** better protection from colds
   - **c.** stronger lungs
5. What is a benefit of valuing nature?
   - **a.** We destroy habitats.
   - **b.** We protect nature.
   - **c.** We do more research.

Read Again and Analyze

Read the text again and respond to the questions. Use evidence from the text to support your responses.

1. **Recognize** In the first paragraph, what main problem does the author discuss? What's the solution?

2. **Examine** How can people who don't live near nature get its benefits?

3. **Illustrate** What is the effect of valuing nature? Name three examples.

4. **Infer** The author writes, "We need to care for nature, so nature can care for us." How does nature care for us?

5. **Relate** What does the quote at the beginning of the article mean? How does it connect to the ideas in the article?

Share Your Perspective

Discuss the questions in a small group.

1. What is the most surprising information from this article? Why?

2. Which benefit is the most important for schools to pay attention to? Why?

3. What other things can you do to reduce stress? Why do you think they help?

Discussion Frames

The most surprising information is …

The most important benefit is … because …

… can also reduce stress. It helps because …

Reflect

How does "Why We Need Nature" help you understand how nature affects us? With a partner, use some of the words to write sentences about the text.

Nouns	Verbs	Adjectives
benefit	concentrate	anxious
disease	protect	mental
health	reduce	physical
peace		
research		
stress		

_____

_____

_____

Wildfires—
Nature's Inferno!

The Angeles National Forest is
engulfed in smoke and flames
during a wildfire, California.

First Thoughts

Which pie chart do you think is correct? Share your reasons with a partner. Then discuss human activity and natural activity that can cause wildfires.

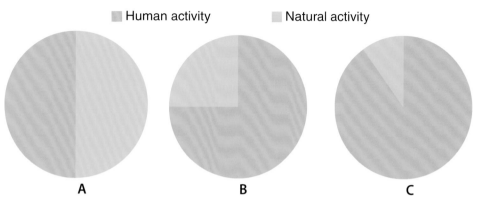

Causes of Wildfires

■ Human activity   ■ Natural activity

A   B   C

Example: *A natural cause is lightning, and a human cause is a campfire.*

Viewing Skill: Take Notes

Take notes to remember important information from a presentation. First, watch and listen for the main ideas. List them in a chart or outline. Then watch again and list the details. Use short phrases.

Apply the Skill

▶ **7.2** Watch the video. Number the main ideas in the correct order. Then write them in a chart on your own paper. Watch again, and add at least two details to explain each main idea.

_____ Effects of wildfires   _____ Three components of wildfires

_____ Causes of wildfires   _____ Where wildfires occur

Understand and Analyze

▶ **7.2** Watch again. Answer the questions. Support your responses with evidence from the video.

1. **Restate** What are wildfires?
2. **Explain** Why are wildfires hard to control?
3. **Recognize** What are the positive and negative effects of wildfires?
4. **Infer** How can wildfires be prevented?

Share Your Perspective

Discuss the questions in a small group.

1. What other natural events have both positive and negative effects?
2. What kinds of weather affect the area you live in? What are the effects?

Discussion Frames

I think … have both negative and positive effects because …

My area is affected by … They cause …

Reflect on the Essential Question

Think about how nature affects us. How does nature make people feel? What does the research show? Write your ideas in the idea web.

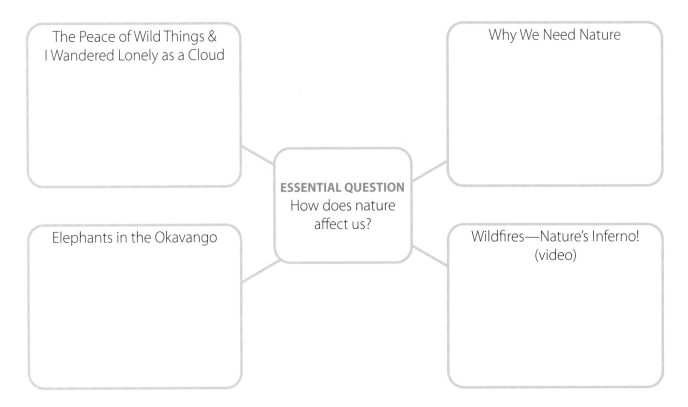

The Peace of Wild Things &
I Wandered Lonely as a Cloud

Why We Need Nature

ESSENTIAL QUESTION
How does nature
affect us?

Elephants in the Okavango

Wildfires—Nature's Inferno!
(video)

Discuss the Essential Question

Look at your ideas about the Essential Question earlier in the unit and your notes above about how nature affects us. How have your ideas about the Essential Question changed? What changed your ideas? Discuss your answers in a group.

Respond to the Essential Question

Write your response to the Essential Question.

Theme Vocabulary

concentrate (v.)
health (n.)
mental (adj.)
peace (n.)
reduce (v.)
stress (n.)

Response Rubric

A good response will

✓ state your opinion
✓ provide support from the texts, the discussion, and your life
✓ use theme vocabulary

_____

_____

_____

Option 1: Write a Poem about Nature

Write a poem to show nature's effect on you.

1. Look at a photo from this unit or take your own photo of nature.

2. Write words and short phrases to describe how it makes you feel.

3. Use your notes to write a poem. Think about the poem's structure. How many stanzas will you use? How many lines in each stanza? Will you use rhyme?

4. Choose words that help your reader "see" the view and understand your feelings.

Read two other poems. Write three words that you liked from each poem. Share your feedback with each poet. After you've shared your poem, show your photo.

Example:

Weeping Cherry Tree

Weeping cherry, is it despair
that your brilliant pink flowers hide?
Your arms reach toward the ground as
if you just want to lie down.

Weeping cherry, your brilliant pink beauty
makes Spring days so bright,
gives darkness light.

Option 2: Design a Research Study

"Why We Need Nature" discusses research studies. Work with a small group. Create your own study to test the effect of nature. Use the example and steps below to guide you.

Example:

Research Question: Are people more physically active when they're outside?	
Group 1: Spend thirty minutes outside (at a park, in a yard, or on a field at school).	**Group 2:** Spend thirty minutes inside (your house, your school, or a library).
Test: Record how many minutes people were doing physical activity (such as walking or running).	
Results: Students who were outside spent more time being physically active.	

1. Write a research question. Use one of these questions, or create your own:
   - Do students remember more definitions of words after looking at photos of nature?
   - Do students report more feelings of happiness after taking a break in nature?

2. Describe two groups for your study. Tell how you will test them.

3. Do your research, and share the results with the class.

Assignment: Develop a Claim

When writing an argument, the author wants to convince the reader to agree with his or her point of view. In this assignment, you will write a paragraph that **develops a claim** with reasons and evidence to support your point of view. You will answer the question: *Should your school provide students with time to experience nature?*

Your paragraph will include the following:

- a title that shares your opinion
- a claim that tells why the school should or shouldn't provide students with time to experience nature
- an idea of how the school can do this
- reasons and evidence to support the claim
- a concluding statement that summarizes your point of view

Explore the Model

Read the model. Look at the author's claim. How does she support it?

Language for Writing

Read the model again.

1. Underline evidence and reasons that support the claim.

2. Notice that the author uses compound and complex sentences. Write the coordinating and subordinating conjunctions below.

Coordinating Conjunctions	Subordinating Conjunctions

3. Authors often use the word *should* to give advice. Complete the sentences below with *should* + a verb or verb phrase from the model.

   Because our school does not have a park or other green space, the school _____ pictures of nature on whiteboards in each classroom.

   In my view, our school _____ to the research and include nature in our daily schedule.

The Perito Moreno Glacier is a glacier located in the Los Glaciares National Park in Santa Cruz Province, Argentina.

Take a Nature Break!

The author's claim states what she believes is true.

The author shares an idea for her school.

The author gives evidence from the article "Why We Need Nature" to support the claim.

"In my view," introduces the concluding statement. It summarizes the author's point of view.

When students have the chance to look at or be in nature, they get a break from the stress of the day and perform better in class. Because our school does not have a park or other green space, the school should show pictures of nature on whiteboards in each classroom. The pictures can stay on the whiteboard until students are seated and teachers are ready to begin. According to the writer Katie Parker, if we look at pictures of nature, our mental health improves. Looking at pictures of nature reduces stress because it allows our brains to rest. As a result, students can concentrate. With this plan, students can get the benefits of nature several times a day, and teachers and students can rest for a short time. Then we will all feel less anxious. We will improve our mood and our learning. Students can share photos of nature from vacations, or they can share other favorite pictures of nature. This will encourage students to take more pictures of nature and value it. In my view, our school should pay attention to the research and include nature in our daily schedule.

Plan Your Writing

Complete the outline.

- Write a claim that tells why the school should or should not provide students with time to experience nature.
- Include an idea of how the school can do this.
- Give evidence and reasons to support your claim.
- Write a concluding statement that summarizes your point of view.
- Write a title for your paragraph.

Outline

Title:
Claim:
Idea for Your School:
Evidence and Reasons:
Concluding Statement:

Write and Revise

Write Use your outline to write a first draft.

- Use subordinating and coordinating conjunctions to connect ideas in sentences.
- Use *should* to share your idea for your school.

Revise Exchange paragraphs with a partner. Using the checklist, review your partner's work and give feedback. Use feedback from your partner to revise your draft.

Feedback Frames

You supported your claim with …

I think you need more details about …

I like the idea for your school because …

☐	Does the author state a claim?
☐	Does the author share an idea for how students can experience nature?
☐	Does the author support the claim with evidence and reasons?
☐	Does the author use conjunctions to connect ideas within sentences?
☐	Does the author include a concluding statement to summarize his or her point of view?

Proofread Check the grammar, spelling, punctuation, and capitalization in your paragraph. Make edits to correct any errors.

TIP

Check that you've punctuated compound and complex sentences correctly. Underline subordinating conjunctions and circle coordinating conjunctions to help you.

Publish

Share your paragraph. Read two of your classmates' paragraphs.

Present Your Claim

You will use your paragraph to create a slideshow and persuade your audience.

Prepare to share your claim:

- Create a slideshow. Write a few short phrases on each slide. Describe your claim, your idea for your school, and your evidence.
- Find pictures to support your argument. Include a picture on all slides if possible.
- Practice giving your presentation. Try not to read from the slides.

Share your presentation with a partner.

- Listen carefully for the claims. How does your partner support them?
- After your partner shares, give feedback. You might say, "You gave three good reasons for why we need nature."

The Laguna de Cube in the forests in Chocó, Ecuador

Protecting the Rainforest in Ecuador 🎧 7.4

EXPLORER IN ACTION

Mónica González is a researcher and conservationist. She works to protect nature.

Mónica González has worked for over thirty years to protect the Chocó rainforest. Her organization, the Foundation for the Conservation of the Tropical Andes (FCAT), focuses on the Mache-Chindul Ecological Reserve in northeast Ecuador. Through research and education, they are documenting and saving the amazing plants and animals in this habitat.

González's work is very important because the Chocó rainforest is in danger. Much of it has been destroyed for its wood and other natural resources. Sadly, only 5% of it remains. Together with local teachers, González's organization teaches the community how to protect this habitat. The programs are having an impact. The communities reduced pollution in the rivers. They planted new trees. A new research station now invites people to visit and learn more about protecting the area. Because of these education efforts and research, the community understands the problems and is now part of the solution.

▶ **7.3** Complete the sentences. Then watch the video to learn more.

1. González works to protect the _____

_____.

2. As a result of her organization, there are _____

_____.

How Will You Take Action?

Choose one or more of these actions to do.

Personal

Go on a virtual nature hike.

1. From home, you can hike the mountains in Switzerland or walk the beaches of Hawaii. Search online for a nature walk, and then choose a place to "wander" around.
2. Explore the area online for 15 to 20 minutes. Take a break, reduce stress, and find pleasure in the sights and sounds of a new place.

School

Persuade your teacher to have class outside. Create a plan and try it out.

1. Create a list of the benefits your class would get from learning outside.
2. Think about how you can do math, English, science, or another subject outside.
3. Create and present a plan. Provide evidence of the benefits and examples of learning outside. Then try your ideas!

Local

Organize a community clean-up day.

1. Invite neighbors, the school community, and local businesses to join you in picking up trash in your community.
2. First, choose a place. Then work with your family, friends, and neighbors to organize the day. Post the event details on a local website.
3. Ask local businesses to give items, such as baked goods, to reward the volunteers. Thank everyone for their service!

Global

Take action to protect a plant or animal.

1. Work to protect a plant or animal near you. For example, the population of the monarch butterfly has dropped by 80%. People are helping to bring the population back by planting milkweed. Monarchs stop, rest, and lay their eggs in these plants.
2. Find out ways you can protect a plant or animal where you live and take action!

Reflect

Reflect on your Take Action project(s). Then complete the sentences.

1. My project(s) was/were successful because _____
   _____.

2. One thing I wish I had done differently is _____
   _____.

3. Because of what I learned in this unit, one thing I will do is _____
   _____.

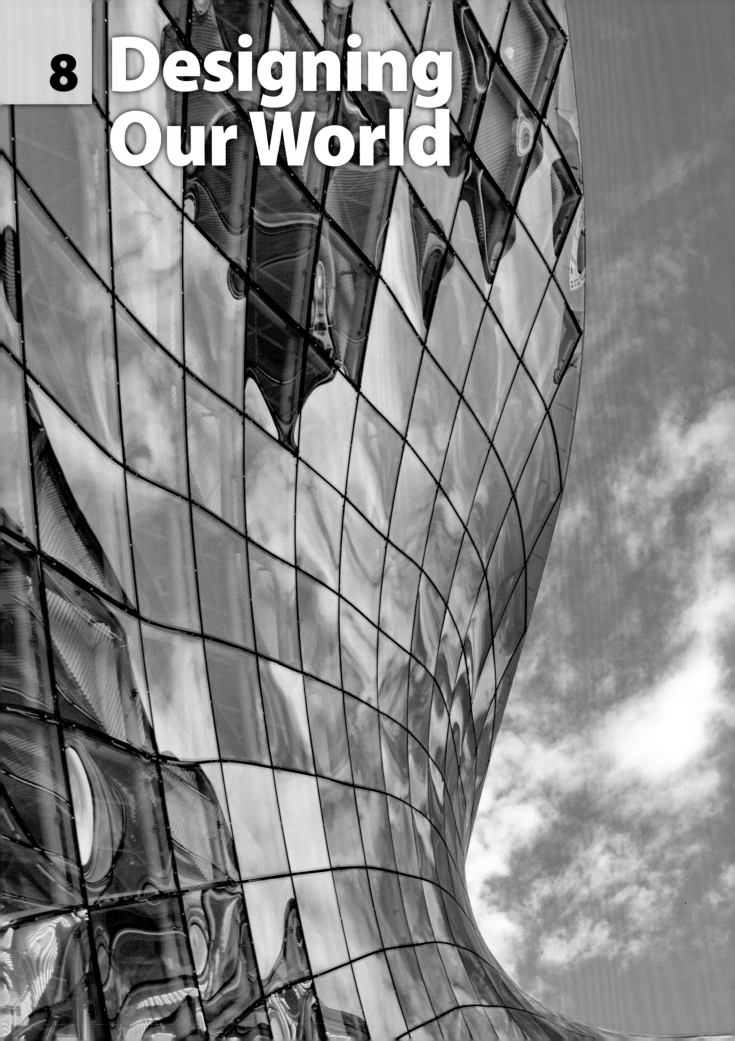

8 Designing Our World

"If I can create some space that people haven't experienced before and if it stays with them or gives them a dream for the future, that's the kind of structure I seek to create."

—TADAO ANDO, JAPANESE ARCHITECT

What does this quote mean to you?

Look at the photo and caption. Discuss the questions.

1. Why do you think the architect designed the building this way?

2. Would you want to visit this shopping mall? Why or why not?

◀ **A shopping mall in Malmö, Sweden**

ESSENTIAL QUESTION
How should we design our world?

Theme Vocabulary

Use these words to express your ideas throughout the unit.

PRACTICE 1 Read the conversation. Think about the meaning of each word in **bold**. Then write each word next to its definition in the chart below.

Do you like our new school?

Yes! The **architect** did a great job. The glass building looks simple and **elegant**. And it has the latest **smart** technology. I love that smartboards record every lesson!

The technology is great and the building is **modern**, but I don't like the **style**. It looks like an art museum instead of a place to learn and have fun. I think an architect should **design** a school that looks beautiful but is also comfortable.

Word	Definition
architect	a person who plans a building or other structure
	to draw or create a plan for something, such as a product or a building
	a particular form or design of something
	controlled by computers and able to do things that seem intelligent
	of or relating to newer things or ideas
	graceful and attractive

PRACTICE 2 Work with a partner. Answer the questions about the conversation.

1. What words describe the style of the school?
2. What smart technology does the school have?
3. How should architects design schools? What are three important features?

Theme Vocabulary

architect (n.)
design (v.)
elegant (adj.)
modern (adj.)
smart (adj.)
style (n.)

Explore the Essential Question

Think Look at the three photos. In which place might you want to live? Imagine you have to describe the place to someone who can't see it. On a piece of paper, write a description of it.

Discuss Read your description, and have a partner guess which photo you are describing. Explain the reasons for your choice.

Respond Circle the words related to design. Add your own ideas. Then use some of the words to complete the sentences below. Share your ideas with a partner.

traditional   elegant   **beautiful**

city   **simple**   **design**   smart technology   **nature**

modern   **safe**

interesting   **exciting**   original

similar

good for the environment

Architects should design buildings that are _____
and_____.
An example of a city I like is _____.
I like it because _____.

Key Vocabulary

PRACTICE Look at the photos and read the sentences. Discuss the meaning of the words in **bold** with a partner. Then ask and answer the questions.

adjust (verb)
He **adjusted** the volume so he could hear the music.
What things in your home can you adjust so you feel more comfortable?

consider (verb)
He **considered** the salads on the menu before he ordered.
What do you consider before you order at a restaurant?

divide (verb)
The garden is **divided** into different areas for each vegetable.
How is your classroom divided?

normal (adjective)
Normal body temperature is 37°C /98°F.
What are other normal signs of good health?

privacy (noun)
The neighbors planted a hedge of trees for **privacy**.
What are other things people do for privacy?

suburbs (noun)
I live in the **suburbs** just forty minutes outside of Boston.
Do you want to live in suburbs or in a city? Why?

Vocabulary: Use a Thesaurus

A **thesaurus** lists synonyms. **Synonyms** are words with similar meanings. Writers use a thesaurus to help them choose the best words and to make their writing interesting. Follow these steps:

1. When you want to describe something, look up a word you know, such as *nice*. Find the definition in the thesaurus that matches your use.

2. Then read the synonyms. Find other, more descriptive words. For example, instead of *nice*, you could use *agreeable*, *pleasant*, or *pretty*.

3. Before you use a synonym, make sure it works in your writing. If you need to, look up its definition and read the example sentence.

Example:

"It was a nice day with a light wind and only a few clouds."

| **Main entry** | Part of speech | Short definition | I find the definition and read the synonyms for *nice* in the thesaurus. I think *pleasant* is a good synonym: *It was a pleasant day with a light wind and only a few clouds.* |

nice (adj.) giving pleasure

Example sentence

A cool glass of lemonade would be nice.

Synonyms for *nice*: *agreeable, pleasant, dreamy, pretty, tasty*

PRACTICE 1 Circle the best synonym for each word in **bold**. Use a thesaurus to help you.

1. It was **lucky** that her new friend lived down the street.
   - **a.** fortunate
   - **b.** happy
   - **c.** successful

2. She was **shaking** a little bit in her sleep. I think she was dreaming.
   - **a.** rattling
   - **b.** twitching
   - **c.** wobbling

3. The nurse spoke to the patient in a **calm** voice.
   - **a.** inactive
   - **b.** soothing
   - **c.** still

PRACTICE 2 Use a thesaurus. List synonyms for each word in **bold** in the sentence.

*The neighbor's cat **ran** across the **grass**.*

ran	grass

ESSENTIAL QUESTION

How should we design our world?

First Thoughts

1. Look at the different types of smart technology for a home.
   Which devices do you want in your home? Discuss with a partner.

Smart Technology for the Home

This smart device learns the temperatures you like and then adjusts the settings.	This smart speaker will send you a text if it hears a fire alarm in your home.	This smart doorbell has a camera and a microphone and can recognize faces.

2. Work with a partner. Create one new idea for smart technology for the home.
   Describe it below. Share your ideas with another pair.

_____

_____

Discuss What's most important for your home? Number the ideas from
1 (most important) to 6 (least important). Then discuss your reasons for your
choices in a small group.

_____ It's safe.   _____ It looks modern.

_____ It has privacy.   _____ It looks beautiful.

_____ There is nature.   _____ It has smart technology.

Reading Skill: Explain Point of View

Authors choose who will **narrate**, or tell, a story. Readers understand the events through the narrator's **point of view**. Use clues to help you identify the point of view in a story and understand how the author develops it.

Point of View	Description	Clues
First-person	A character in the story narrates what happens. The reader only learns about this character's thoughts and feelings.	Look for first-person pronouns (*I/me/mine/myself*) in sentences that describe the narrator's experiences.
Third-person	The story is narrated by someone outside the story. The reader learns about the events and the thoughts and feelings of one or more characters.	Look for the characters' names and third-person pronouns (*he/his, she/her, they/their*) in sentences that describe the thoughts and feelings of a character or characters.

Skill in Action

Read the paragraph from *Rickshaw Girl* (in Unit 6) and a reader's thoughts. Underline clues that help the reader figure out the point of view. Then discuss with a partner. What is the point of view? What do we learn from the narrator?

A narrator describes the events in the story, but the narrator is not part of the story.

One day Father surprised them by coming home early for lunch. "The rickshaw's looking worse than ever," he said. "It's starting to rust. And Hassan's shop should be open for business by now. I'll go there today, and if it's open, I'll price the repairs."

I can understand the characters through their dialogue. These are the words the characters say.

"But … have you earned enough money, Father?" Naima asked, even though she knew the answer.

Naima doesn't say this question aloud. She thinks it to herself.

The narrator describes what Naima is thinking.

The idea came wheeling into her mind as though it had been waiting for the chance. She was still the best alpana painter in the village, wasn't she?

Read and answer the question: **What smart technology does the Bells'
house have?** As you read, underline any parts of the text you have questions
about or find confusing.

The Smart House

from **Eager**
by **Helen Fox**

1   The Bell Family lived in the **suburbs**, in a house built of glass
and steel, **designed** by Mr. Bell. Their neighbors in Wynston
Avenue, who also lived in glass houses, had planted tall hedges to
hide them from view. Mr. and Mrs. Bell said what was the point of
5   a beautiful house if no one else could enjoy it, and built themselves
a low brick wall. However, they liked their **privacy** as much as
anyone, and it was fortunate that the house stood alone on a bend
in the road. There was also a huge lime tree in the front garden
that covered one side of the building.

10   The center of the house was an atrium,[1] paved with brick and
full of plants and flowers. A wide hallway opening onto it connected
the ground-floor rooms. There was a half-landing with an office,
exercise room and study area; bedrooms and bathrooms were on the
top floor. The land at the back was **divided** into grass, a vegetable
15   garden and a slightly wild overgrown patch at the far end.

As dawn approached, the birds in the lime tree began their
singing. A gray cat slinked across the lawn and over the brick
wall. Seconds later the house swept a sensor[2] around the garden
for the hundredth time that night to check for intruders.[3] It took
20   the outside temperature and barometric pressure.[4] Today was
going to be a mild day with the possibility of a light shower
before the evening.

> **STOP & THINK**
> **Infer** What is Mr. Bell's
> job? What else do
> you know about the
> Bell family from the
> description of their
> house?

---

[1] **atrium** wide, open area with a glass ceiling
[2] **sensor** device that detects heat, light, sound, and motion and responds
[3] **intruders** people who enter a place they are not allowed
[4] **barometric pressure** weight of the air

A noise downstairs alerted the house that someone was up.
It turned on its electronic eye in the kitchen and saw that the cook
was at work. He was chopping something on a large wooden
board and talking to the kettle.

Room by room, the house checked on the family members.
Fleur Bell was buried so deeply under the covers that it was
impossible to tell which way up she was. The house zoomed
in somewhere about her middle to reassure itself that she was
still breathing. Satisfied that the blanket was gently rising and
falling, the house turned its eye to the bedroom next door. Fleur's
younger brother, Gavin Bell, was sprawled across the bed, the
covers thrown off as if he had been wrestling in his sleep. **Normal**,
concluded the house quickly, with barely a glance at him.

Charlotte Bell, lying in a cot in the nursery, was twitching in
her sleep. No cause for alarm there. In the main bedroom Mr. and
Mrs. Bell looked comfortable enough, but Mr. Bell was muttering[5]
to himself and the house **considered** that he might have a fever.
It looked for other symptoms,[6] found none, and decided that he
was nearing the end of a dream cycle.

The hours passed and the house grew busier—waking
everyone up and setting the temperature for showers and baths.
It checked the go-between[7] for news that might interest the Bells,
adjusted roof panels to create more heat and raised the blinds on
the day ahead.

STOP & THINK
Conclude What do
you think the house's
electronic eye is?

---

[5] **muttering** talking quietly
[6] **symptoms** changes in the body that show you are sick
[7] **go-between** word used in this story for a future device like the internet

Gavin was the first to come downstairs. He was in a bad mood, though he didn't know why. It felt as if his body had been given a good shake and parts of him had fallen back into the

50 wrong place. He had been looking forward to today. After home study he was going to the learning center for a game of liveball. That was the good part. On the other hand, he was sure he had instructed the house to wake him with his favorite music; instead, a shrill[8] voice had screeched[9] "Wakey! Wakey!" in his ear. He

55 hadn't had breakfast yet, and he had a nagging[10] feeling that his mum and dad were going to have one of their Discussions. He jumped the final steps and burst into the dining room, his shirt half undone and one of his socks twisted.

"Where is everyone?"

60 "Your mother is in the shower and your father is changing Charlotte's diaper," replied the house in a soothing, feminine voice. "Your sister is—"

"All right," snapped Gavin. "I didn't really expect an answer. It was a rit … ret …"

65 "Rhetorical question[11]?" prompted the house.

"Yes, I know." Gavin sat down to adjust his sock. "Anyway, you're not supposed to be on in here. You know Mum doesn't like machines in the dining room."

"I am not a machine," corrected the house.

---

[8] **shrill** very loud and high pitched
[9] **screeched** screamed
[10] **nagging** worried
[11] **rhetorical question** asking a question to show how you feel, not to get an answer

STOP & THINK
Analyze Word Choice Consider the words *shrill* and *screeched*. How does Gavin feel about the house waking him up?

About the Author (b. 1962)
Helen Fox was a teacher and actress before she became a writer. This excerpt comes from her first book.

Close Read

Work with a partner.

1. Determine the meanings of your underlined words and phrases.

2. Discuss the question:

   What smart technology does the Bells' house have?

Understand

Is the idea important to the Bells? Check (✓) *Yes, No,* or *Not Given* if the text doesn't discuss the idea.

Is the idea important to the Bells?	Yes	No	Not Given
1. They need complete privacy from their neighbors.	☐	☐	☐
2. The house is beautiful.	☐	☐	☐
3. The house is safe from intruders.	☐	☐	☐
4. The house doesn't use a lot of energy.	☐	☐	☐
5. There is nature, such as plants, trees, and flowers.	☐	☐	☐
6. The house is divided into separate rooms.	☐	☐	☐

Apply the Skill: Explain Point of View

PRACTICE 1 Write sentences from "The Smart House." Underline the clues in each sentence that help you understand the point of view.

1. Write a sentence that describes the house's actions.

   _____

   _____

2. Write a sentence that describes a family member's actions.

   _____

   _____

3. Write a sentence that describes a character's thoughts or feelings.

   _____

   _____

PRACTICE 2 Circle the correct answers to complete the sentences about point of view.

"The Smart House" uses *first-person / third-person* point of view. The narrator *is / is not* a character in the story. The narrator *tells / does not tell* the reader about Gavin's thoughts and feelings.

Read Again and Analyze

Read the text again and respond to the questions. Use evidence from the text to support your responses.

1. **Infer** What is the setting—the time and place—of the story? How do you know?

2. **Recognize** What does the house know?

3. **Deduce** How do Gavin and the house feel about each other? How do you know?

4. **Illustrate** The house says, "I am not a machine." Give two examples to support its statement and two examples to support Gavin's description of it as a machine.

5. **Examine** Do the Bells have privacy from the house? Why or why not?

Share Your Perspective

Discuss the questions in a small group.

1. There are many positive aspects of smart technology. What are some negative aspects?

2. How is smart technology different from a person? Is the Bells' house a machine?

3. Do you want to live in a home like the Bells' house? Why or why not?

Discussion Frames

Some negative aspects of smart technology are …

One way smart technology is different is … Another way is …

I want/don't want to … because …

Reflect

How does "The Smart House" help you understand how we should design our world? With a partner, use some of the words to write sentences about the story.

Nouns	Verbs	Adjectives
architect	adjust	elegant
privacy	consider	modern
style	design	normal
suburbs	divide	smart

_____

_____

_____

Examine the Photo

1. Look at the photo. Describe what you see.

2. Where do you think this photo was taken? What is happening? Give evidence to support your opinion.

3. Write three questions about the photo. Discuss your questions with a small group.

Find Out ▶ 8.1

Watch photographer Luca Locatelli talk about his photo.

1. Did he answer any of your questions? Which ones?

2. Where was this photo taken? What is happening?

3. Why was this built here?

4. Why did Luca take this photo?

Reflect

What does this photo suggest about how we should design our world? What other old or empty structures could we reuse? How could we reuse them?

Share Your Story

1. Take or find a photo that shows an interesting building or design that you feel fits into a well-designed world.

2. Take or find another photo that shows a building or design that you don't like.

3. Tell your classmates about the photos. Explain your opinions.

ABOUT THE PHOTOGRAPHER

Luca Locatelli takes photographs that explore the relationship between people, technology, and the environment.

Key Vocabulary

PRACTICE Look at the photos and read the sentences. Discuss the meaning of the words in **bold** with a partner. Then ask and answer the questions.

artistic (adjective)
She has a lot of **artistic** talent.
What skills do artistic people have?

create (verb)
I like to **create** comics.
What do you like to create?

complicated (adjective)
This math problem is very **complicated**.
Do you like to do complicated math problems?

incredible (adjective)
The sunset was **incredible**!
What incredible place have you seen?

passion (noun)
They have a lot of **passion** for their team.
What do you have a lot of passion for?

social (adjective)
The tables in our classroom allow us to be **social**.
Do you like being social in class?

Grammar: Comparative and Superlative Adjectives

We use **comparative adjectives** to compare one person, place, or thing to another.

*The hotel is **taller** than the museum.*

We use **superlative adjectives** to compare one person, place, or thing to a group.

*The hotel is **the tallest** building in the city.*

Rules	Adjective	Comparative	Superlative
For adjectives with one syllable, add -er / the + -est.	tall	taller	the tallest
For adjectives with two syllables ending in y, change the y to i and add -er / the + -est.	pretty	prettier	the prettiest
For adjectives with two or more syllables, use more + adjective / the + most + adjective.	famous	more famous	the most famous
Some adjectives don't follow the rules.	good	better	the best
	bad	worse	the worst

PRACTICE 1 Complete the chart for each adjective.

Adjective	Comparative	Superlative
1. social		
2. elegant		
3. complicated		
4. busy		
5. small		

PRACTICE 2 Complete each sentence with the correct comparative or superlative form of each adjective from the chart in Practice 1.

1. The house was _____ home in the suburbs. It had only one bedroom.

2. Our new sofa looks _____ than our old sofa, but it's not as comfortable.

3. People are _____ in gym class than in other classes. It's easier to talk and move around.

4. Yesterday, the store was _____ than today. Customers waited in long lines.

5. The game was _____ one we played. It had so many rules.

ESSENTIAL QUESTION

How should we design our world?

First Thoughts

Look at the photos and read the descriptions of the schools. Compare the schools with a partner. What adjectives best describe each school? Discuss which school you like best.

DAVID FRUTOS / Fotografía

| Evelyn Grace Academy in the United Kingdom has four schools for students of different ages so that students can stay in their community as they get older. Students enter the building by running down the track. | Nanyang Primary School in Singapore uses fun, bright colors. There is a large, open area in the middle of the school for students to spend time outside and be active and social. | The buildings in this elementary school in Roldán, Spain, are covered in fake grass. This protects them from heavy rain and makes the school look like it is part of the natural world. |

Discuss Check (✓) the statements you agree with. Then discuss your answers with a group.

☐ A building should help people be social.

☐ The design of a beautiful building is usually complicated.

☐ Buildings are better when they look like the natural world.

☐ Buildings should be original and not look like other buildings.

☐ Architects are artists. Buildings are art.

Reading Skill: Use Text Evidence to Make Inferences

Authors don't explain everything directly in a text. Sometimes you need to make an **inference**, or an educated guess. As you read, use **text evidence**—details, examples, and facts—along with what you know to make inferences about the text. Follow these steps:

1. Read the details in the text. This is the text evidence.
2. Think about the information in the text. Think about what you already know from your experience.
3. Then make an inference about the text.

Skill in Action

Read the paragraphs from "The Queen of the Curve" and a reader's inferences. Then look at the text evidence. Complete the inference below about Zaha Hadid with your thoughts.

> The text says the school was one of the best in the world. I know it's hard to get into a really good school. I think Zaha was very smart.

Zaha studied mathematics at university—an important subject if you want to become an architect. And then she moved to London, to study at the Architectural Association School of Architecture—one of the best schools in the world.

> I've never heard descriptions like these before. I think Zaha was very creative and an original thinker.

When she graduated, she was described as "a planet in her own inimitable orbit" and "the inventor of the 89 degrees," because nothing was ever at 90 degrees for her. Details did not interest her: her mind was always focused on the "big picture." For example, Zaha's student project was a painting of a hotel on a bridge. Doesn't it sound incredible?

> I know most architecture students create buildings, not paintings, for their final project. I think _____ _____ _____

Read and answer the question: **How does the author describe Zaha Hadid's style of architecture?** As you read, underline any parts of the text you have questions about or find confusing.

The Queen of the Curve

from **Amazing Women of the Middle East**
by **Wafa' Tarnowska**

Guangzhou Opera House, Guangzhou, China

∩ 8.2

1   "The Queen of the Curve": that's what they called Zaha Hadid, who became the most famous female **architect** in the world. Her first name means "proud" in Arabic, and her surname "iron." With a name like this, Zaha Hadid was sure to become an
5   outstanding[1] woman!

     Zaha won many awards in her lifetime. She was the first woman ever to receive the Royal Gold Medal from the Royal Institute of British Architects on her own (RIBA Stirling Prize).

     With her team, she worked on nine hundred and fifty projects
10   in forty-four countries. Museums, bridges, ski jumps, sports centers, airports, opera houses, hotels, and office blocks—there was nothing she did not try! So how did this woman become a leader in the world of architecture?

---

[1] **outstanding** excellent

" *The goal posts might shift, but you should have a goal.* **"**

               –Zaha Hadid

Zaha had known since she was eleven that she wanted to be an architect. Her mother, Wajiha, was an artist, her brother a writer, and her father a wealthy man. This meant that travel and an international education were possible for Zaha. She went to boarding schools[2] in England and Switzerland, and we know that trips to ancient Sumerian cities left an impression[3] on her.

Zaha studied mathematics at university—an important subject if you want to become an architect. And then she moved to London, to study at the Architectural Association School of Architecture—one of the best schools in the world.

When she graduated, she was described as "a planet in her own inimitable orbit" and "the inventor of the 89 degrees," because nothing was ever at 90 degrees for her. Details did not interest her: her mind was always focused on the "big picture." For example, Zaha's student project was a painting of a hotel on a bridge. Doesn't it sound **incredible**?

After she finished university, Zaha worked in the Netherlands, but when she became a British citizen in 1980, she opened her own company, Zaha Hadid Architects (ZHA), introducing people to new forms of architecture: **elegant**, inspirational, and colorful. She drew hundreds of sketches by hand, very quickly for each project without a computer.

At first, her sketches were mainly published in architectural journals but remained unbuilt. One of her first designs won a competition for the Opera House of Cardiff in Wales. But the Welsh government found another architect. This did not stop Zaha from sketching and sharing her exciting new ideas with audiences around the world.

> **STOP & THINK**
> **Conclude** What skills, experiences, and talents does an architect need?

---

[2] **boarding schools** schools where students live
[3] **impression** effect on someone's thoughts

In 1988, she was chosen to show her drawings and paintings at MOMA, New York's Museum of **Modern** Art. She also taught at leading architecture schools while taking her **passion** to places few dared to go: Zaha's creations are "out for a virtual[4] dance," because she knows how to make "dream places real." In 2004, she became the first woman to win the Pritzker Architecture Prize, which is the most respected award in architecture. What an achievement!

45

---

[4] **virtual** almost or nearly something

The main auditorium of the Guangzhou Opera House

So where can you see Zaha's buildings? Well, you could go
to the Queen Elizabeth Olympic Park, site of the London 2012
Olympics, where the amazing Aquatics Centre sits as a dream
place made real! With its swooping curves, you wonder how it was
possible to **create** such a building. The good news is that since the
Olympics, it has been open for everyone to enjoy both swimming
and diving. Another incredible building is the Eli and Edythe Broad
Art Museum at Michigan State University. With so many angles
in steel and glass, it takes your breath away! She also **designed**
bridges: the wonderful Sheikh Zayed Bridge, between the island of
Abu Dhabi and the mainland, looks like waves. Some say it is one of
the most **complicated** bridges that has ever been built.

Zaha also loved designing objects for everyday life and was
interested in giving architecture a **social** goal. She believed that
part of an architect's job is to make people feel good where
they live or work and for children to enjoy their school spaces.
Her Z-shaped school in Brixton (in London), the Evelyn Grace
Academy, won her a second Stirling Prize.

STOP & THINK
Infer What are other
examples of social goals
of architecture?

Her main advice for young people was "to be very focused
and work very hard," because "working on an architecture project
means perseverance.[5]"

She also believed that architects were real artists, and she
wasn't afraid to be funny, honest, and show her emotions.
Sometimes she felt as if she was the only woman architect, but
mostly she did not mind: "It's okay, I like being on the edge.[6]"

On March 31, 2016, Zaha died of a heart attack. The world
was shocked. A square was named after her in Belgium, the "Zaha
Hadidplein," in front of the Antwerp Port House she had added
on to. Her outstanding buildings and designs show her creativity
and **artistic** talent.

---

[5] **perseverance** determination
[6] **on the edge** a risk-taker

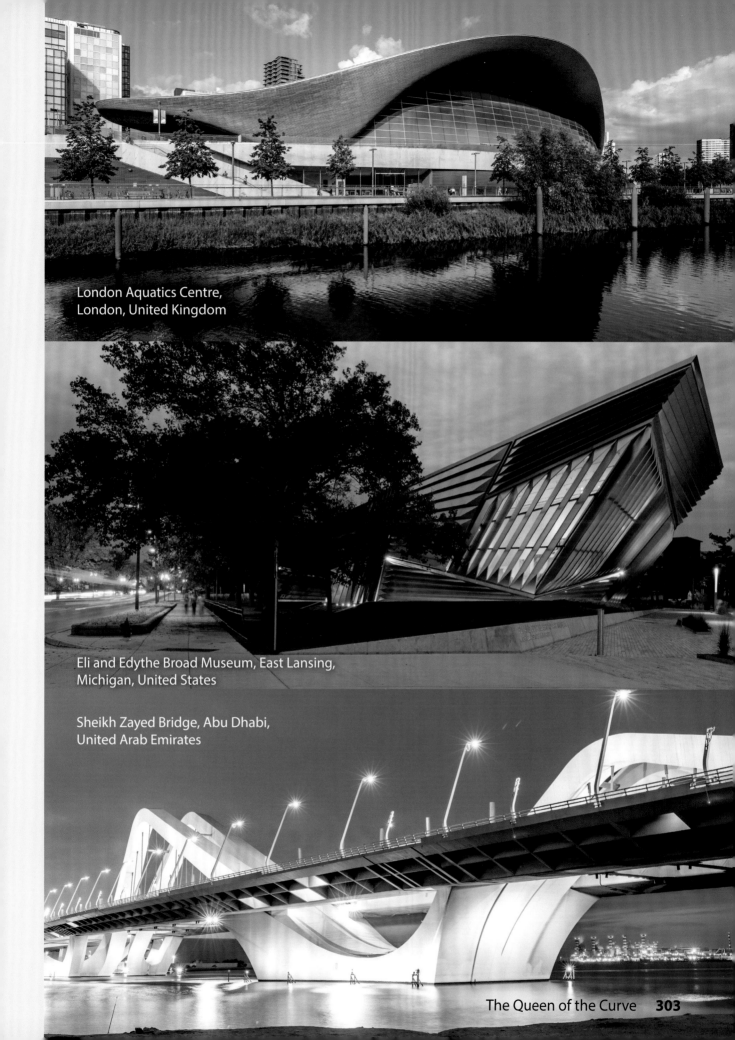

London Aquatics Centre,
London, United Kingdom

Eli and Edythe Broad Museum, East Lansing,
Michigan, United States

Sheikh Zayed Bridge, Abu Dhabi,
United Arab Emirates

Close Read

Work with a partner.

1. Determine the meanings of your underlined words and phrases.

2. Discuss the question:

   How does the author describe Zaha Hadid's style of architecture?

Understand

Read the summary. Three sentences have incorrect information. Correct the mistakes.

As a young person, Zaha Hadid traveled internationally and had an excellent education. She studied art at one of the best schools in the world. For her student project, she created an incredible painting. After graduation, she drew sketches and her work was built. Her paintings and drawings were displayed in an art museum. She became respected for her designs. The Sheikh Zayed Bridge is one of the most elegant bridges ever built. Her buildings look impossible to build. They show her creativity and her social goals. She wanted people to enjoy her buildings.

Apply the Skill: Use Text Evidence to Make Inferences

PRACTICE 1 Check (✔) two inferences that the text supports. Then circle evidence from the text for each inference that you checked.

1. _____ Zaha Hadid had a difficult time getting her designs for architecture built.

2. _____ It was not common for a woman to be an award-winning architect.

3. _____ Zaha Hadid's paintings were more important than her architecture.

PRACTICE 2 Write your own inference. List the text evidence.

My inference: _____

Text evidence: _____

_____

Read Again and Analyze

Read the text again and respond to the questions. Use evidence from the text to support your responses.

1. **Examine** What was Zaha Hadid's passion throughout her life? What examples best show it?

2. **Illustrate** What was Hadid's goal for architecture? Give an example of one of her buildings, and describe how it meets her goal.

3. **Recognize** (Lines 68–69) Hadid said "working on an architecture project means perseverance." How did she show perseverance?

4. **Relate** (Lines 72–73) Hadid said, "It's okay, I like being on the edge." How does her life's work show that she was "on the edge"?

5. **Compare** What do Hadid's projects have in common?

Share Your Perspective

Discuss the questions in a small group.

1. Do you like Zaha Hadid's style of architecture? Why or why not?

2. What three goals should an architect have?

3. How might buildings in the future be different from now?

Reflect

How does "The Queen of the Curve" help you understand how we should design our world? With a partner, use some of the words to write sentences about the text.

Nouns	Verbs	Adjectives
architect passion style	create design	artistic complicated elegant incredible modern smart social

_____

_____

_____

_____

Discussion Frames

In my opinion, Zaha Hadid's style is …

One goal of an architect should be …

Buildings in the future might be different because they will …

A Self-Cooling Building Inspired by Bugs

A termite mound

First Thoughts

▶ **8.2** Look at the photos and read the captions. Discuss the questions with a partner. Then watch the video and check your answers.

1. How is the Eastgate Center like a termite mound?

2. Why would an architect want to design a building to be like nature?

Viewing Skill: Use Visuals to Understand Key Ideas

When you watch a video, use the visuals to help you understand the important ideas. Listen to the description and ask yourself: *What ideas about the topic does this visual show? What can I better understand from the visual?*

Eastgate Centre Building, Harare, Zimbabwe

Apply the Skill

▶ **8.2** Read the ideas below. Match the description to each idea. Watch the video again to check your answers.

1. _____ how air flows in a termite mound

2. _____ how cool air moves in the building

3. _____ how concrete blocks affect the air

4. _____ how warm air is released

a. The air rises and leaves through the ceiling and chimneys.

b. Tiny holes let air pass through.

c. Fans pull in the air and disperse it.

d. They absorb the cold air and keep it cool.

Understand and Analyze

Answer the questions. Support your responses with evidence from the video. Watch the video again if necessary.

1. **Summarize** What was Mick Pearce's problem? How did he solve it?
2. **Paraphrase** What is biomimicry?
3. **Compare** How does the building cool itself like a termite mound?
4. **Recognize** What are two positive effects of this cooling system?

Share Your Perspective

Discuss the questions in a small group.

1. If you could use nature to design a building, what would be your inspiration? Why? How would the building mimic nature?

2. What are other ideas for designing buildings that use less energy?

Discussion Frames

I would use … for inspiration because …

Another idea for a building to use less energy is …

Reflect on the Essential Question

Think about how the architects in this unit designed their buildings.
Write your ideas in the idea web.

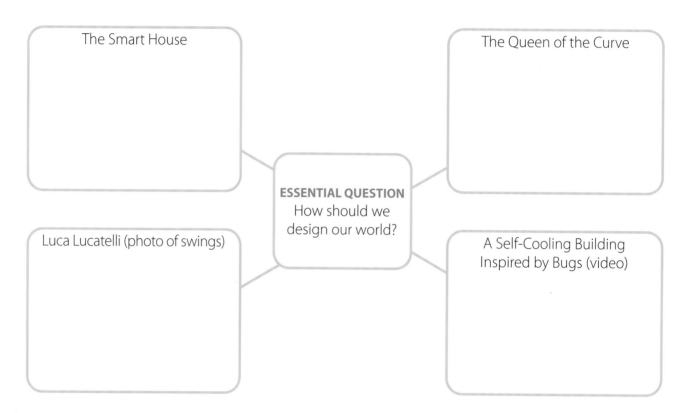

The Smart House

The Queen of the Curve

ESSENTIAL QUESTION
How should we
design our world?

Luca Lucatelli (photo of swings)

A Self-Cooling Building
Inspired by Bugs (video)

Discuss the Essential Question

Look at your ideas about the Essential Question earlier in the unit and your
notes in the idea web above. How have your ideas about the Essential
Question changed? What changed your ideas? Discuss your answers in a group.

Respond to the Essential Question

Write your response to the Essential Question.

Response Rubric
A good response will
✓ state your opinion
✓ provide support from the texts, the discussion, and your life
✓ use theme vocabulary

Theme Vocabulary

architect (n.)
design (v.)
elegant (adj.)
modern (adj.)
smart (adj.)
style (n.)

Option 1: Design Your Perfect School

Work with a partner. Design the perfect school.

1. Write three goals for the design of your school. Consider different ways to achieve the goals. Then decide on your plan.

2. Create a physical model or draw a picture to show the different parts of the school.

3. Present your school to the class. Share your goals. Describe the building. Invite your class to share feedback on how your school achieves your goals.

Example:

Our first goal was to create a school that provides outdoor spaces for students to be in nature. We also wanted a fun environment so students would be excited to go to school. And like Zaha Hadid, we wanted to create an incredible building to inspire students and make them feel good.

Option 2: Rewrite and Extend the Text

Imagine "The Smart House" was told in first person from the house's point of view. How would the story be different?

1. Rewrite the story to use first-person point of view. Narrate only the house's thoughts, feelings, and actions. Include details to show what it thinks about Gavin and the other family members.

2. Predict what happens after the house says, "I am not a machine." Create a new ending that extends the text and shows the house's point of view.

	The House's Thoughts, Feelings, and Actions	The House's Words
Beginning	*I heard a noise downstairs and quickly turned on my eye. I saw the cook chopping something …*	*"Okay, totally normal," I whispered to myself.*
Middle		
End		

Assignment: Write an Introduction to a Story

In fiction stories, the writer creates the setting, the characters, and the plot. In this assignment, you will write the **introduction** (three paragraphs) for a story about waking up in a different world.

Your paragraphs will include the following:

- a title to interest your reader
- a paragraph to introduce the main character(s) and the setting
- two paragraphs to describe the setting
- a third-person narrator to describe the characters' thoughts, feelings, and actions

Explore the Model

Read the model. Look at how the writer developed the story elements. What details best help you understand who the character is and where and when the story takes place?

Language for Writing

Read the model again.

1. Which words and phrases best describe the world? Share your answers with a partner.

2. In the model, find three comparative forms of adjectives and two superlative forms. Write them in the chart.

Comparative Adjectives	Superlative Adjectives

3. Answer the questions to identify how the writer introduces the character and setting.

   Who is the main character? What do you know about her?

   _____

   _____

   What is the setting? What does it look like?

   _____

   _____

   _____

The title
interests the
reader.

The Future Forest

The first
paragraph
introduces
the main
character and
the setting
of the story.
The setting
changes from
the suburbs
to a forest.

Miriam wakes up and looks at the clock: 7:00 a.m. She jumps out of bed. School starts in thirty minutes. She gets ready fast. Then she opens the door and gasps. It is the most incredible view of a forest. These are the tallest trees that she has ever seen, and she is in one of them! She takes a slow step forward and carefully looks over the balcony. It's a long way down to the ground. She can see a river's winding path. This is NOT her home in the suburbs!

Descriptive
adjectives
help the
reader picture
the setting.

She quickly turns around and looks at the house. It doesn't look like a kid's tree house. It's modern. Curved glass circles the tree. The house is small but elegant. There can't be much privacy with all that glass. However, when she takes a closer look, the glass changes color. She can't see inside. It's like the house knew she was

The narrator
describes the
character's
thoughts.

looking at it. She thinks back. What did it look like on the inside? She can't remember. She looks for the door but can't find it. That's weird. How did she come out? Her heart begins to pound, but then she feels the cool air on her face. She hears birdsong. She turns around and looks at the view. She begins to feel better.

In the last
paragraph,
the narrator
gives details
to describe
the larger
world
beyond the
house.

That's when she realizes it. She's not alone. Underneath the branches thick with leaves, she sees another glass house. There are more, maybe hundreds of homes. Some of them wrap around the trees. Others look more dangerous. They dangle from the branches. They swing in the breeze. She's living in a city in the trees, a forest of the future!

Plan Your Writing

Complete the outline.

- Think of a character (or characters). Who is the character? What is his or her normal life like?
- What does the character see in the new world when he or she wakes up? Describe the new world. What is it like? Describe the character's thoughts.
- Draw a picture of the new world.
- Add a title that helps describe something original or unique about your story.

Outline

Title:
Character(s):
Setting 1 (normal life):
Setting 2 (new world):
Character's thoughts:
Picture:

Write and Revise

Write Use your outline to write a first draft.

- Use a thesaurus to find descriptive words.
- Use comparative and superlative adjectives to describe the new world.

Revise Exchange paragraphs with a partner. Using the checklist, review your partner's work and give feedback. Use feedback from your partner to revise your draft.

☐ Does the writer include an interesting title?

☐ Does the first paragraph introduce the character and setting?

☐ Do the second and third paragraphs describe the new world?

☐ Does the writer use adjectives and details to help the reader "see" the world?

☐ Does the narrator tell about the character's thoughts and feelings?

Proofread Check the grammar, spelling, punctuation, and capitalization in your writing. Make edits to correct any errors.

TIP

Check that you've used the correct forms of comparative and superlative adjectives. Underline comparative and superlative adjectives. Check their spellings.

Publish

Share your writing about waking up in a different world. Read two of your classmates' paragraphs.

Present Your Introduction to a Story

You will record your paragraphs for your classmates to listen to.

Prepare to share your paragraphs:

- Underline descriptive details. Read these slowly so readers can create pictures in their minds.
- Circle words that are difficult for you to pronounce. Practice saying these words before you record.
- Practice reading aloud, using your voice to show your character's feelings.

Record your work.

- Post your audio to a class website.
- Listen to five of your classmates' recordings. Write one thing you like about each. Then share the feedback and discuss your different worlds.

Living root bridge in Meghalaya, India

Growing Living Bridges in India 🎧 8.3

EXPLORER IN ACTION
Sanjeev Shankar
is an architect, researcher, and innovator.

Sanjeev Shankar was born in southern India and studied architecture, design, and science. Along with his training, he uses nature and traditional knowledge to create designs that have a positive impact on our world.

One of Shankar's projects focuses on Meghalaya, in Northeast India. The local communities of this region have long used the roots of the Indian rubber tree to form living bridges. These bridges are up to approximately 174 feet long, and some have lasted for hundreds of years.

These living bridges are home to different plants and animals. Additionally, they improve the soil and help protect the land from erosion, landslides, and floods. Finally, they bring people to the region, which helps the local economy. However, these bridges are being replaced with new structures. Shankar works with the local community, scientists, and the government to conserve these incredible bridges, and restore the surrounding natural environment.

▶ 8.3 Complete the sentences. Then watch the video to learn more.

1. Three benefits of the living bridges are _____

_____

2. I think another positive impact the living bridges will have is

_____

How Will You Take Action?

Choose one or more of these actions to do.

Personal

Improve an everyday object.

1. Think about something you use every day, such as gloves, a spoon, or a bookbag.
2. How can you improve its design? Can you make it more exciting, comfortable, or elegant?
3. Create a design and try it out!

School

Redesign your classroom.

1. First, evaluate its design. Does it allow students to be social? Is it a nice place to learn? How does it make you feel?
2. Work in a small group. Create a design to change your classroom.
3. Share your designs with the class. Decide which ideas might work.

Local

Evaluate the design of your community.

1. Research shows that people who live near grocery stores and nature have better health. What other things do healthy communities have? Create a list.
2. As a class, vote on the top five items for a healthy community.
3. Then evaluate your community. How can it be improved? Write an email to the local newspaper to share your ideas.

Global

Take a virtual tour of a city, and then make a tour of your city.

1. Take a virtual tour of a city you've never been to. Consider what makes the tour special.
2. Then work with a group. Create a video to show some of the great places in your city or community.
3. Post your videos for a class in another country to see and explore.

Reflect

Reflect on your Take Action project(s). Then complete the sentences.

1. My project(s) was/were successful because _____
   _____ .

2. One thing I wish I had done differently is _____
   _____ .

3. Because of what I learned in this unit, one thing I will do is _____
   _____ .

Theme vocabulary words are noted in blue.

A

able *(adj.)* having the power or skill to do something

adjust *(v.)* to change or move something so that it works better

alive *(adj.)* living; not dead

alone *(adj.)* not involving anyone or anything else; by oneself

anxious *(adj.)* feeling nervous or afraid about something

architect *(n.)* a person who plans, draws, or models a building or other structure

artist *(n.)* a person who creates art, such as drawings, paintings, sculpture, etc.

artistic *(adj.)* having the skills of an artist; showing imagination

audience *(n.)* a group of people who watch or listen to something

awkward *(adj.)* causing embarrassment; uncomfortable

B

badly *(adv.)* in a bad manner or way

become *(v.)* to begin to be or come to be something

believe *(v.)* to think something is true

benefit *(n.)* a good effect or result

borrow *(v.)* to get something from someone and use it before returning it

bother *(v.)* to cause to feel upset or worried

C

cause *(v.)* to make something happen

chance *(n.)* the possibility that something may happen; an opportunity

cheer *(v.)* to shout with joy or excitement

clear *(adj.)* easily understood; with no doubts

collect *(v.)* to bring or get things together from different places

communicate *(v.)* to exchange information by using words and/or gestures

complicated *(adj.)* having many connected parts

concentrate *(v.)* to focus one's attention on something

concert *(n.)* a public performance of music or dance

confusing *(adj.)* hard to understand

consider *(v.)* to think carefully about something before deciding

continue *(v.)* to keep doing something

cool *(adj.)* appealing in a way that others approve of; suggesting acceptance or agreement

correct *(adj.)* having no errors; right

create *(v.)* to make something new using your imagination

creative *(adj.)* having the ability to make new things or think of new ideas

crowd *(n.)* a large group of people gathered together in one place

culture *(n.)* the shared beliefs of a particular group of people; the way a group of people lives and acts

D

dangerous *(adj.)* able to cause harm; involving danger

dead *(adj.)* not alive; no longer having life

decide *(v.)* to make a choice about something

decision *(n.)* a choice you make after thinking about it

design *(v.)* to draw or create a plan for something, such as a product or a building

despair *(n.)* a feeling of being very sad or without hope

determined *(adj.)* feeling strongly that you are going to do something and that nothing will stop you

differently *(adv.)* in a way that is not the same

disagree *(v.)* to not have the same opinion or idea

disaster *(n.)* something that has a bad result; a failure

discover *(v.)* to find or see something for the first time

disease *(n.)* an illness that affects someone or something

divide *(v.)* to separate into different parts

E

effect *(n.)* a change resulting from an event or action

elegant *(adj.)* graceful and attractive

empathy *(n.)* the feeling that you understand and share another person's feelings

encourage *(v.)* to make someone feel hopeful; to give support and courage to someone

entertainment *(n.)* something that is pleasing or enjoyable

excitement *(n.)* a feeling of great interest; a feeling of being excited

expect *(v.)* to think that something will happen

experience *(n.)* something that happens to you that affects how you feel or act

experiment *(n.)* a test you can do to learn something

F

familiar *(adj.)* knowing something because it has been seen or heard before

figure out *(v. phr.)* to find an answer or solution to something; to solve

form *(v.)* to cause something to happen; to bring together

frustrated *(adj.)* being upset because you are not able to do something

G

give up *(v. phr.)* to stop doing something

global *(adj.)* involving the whole world

goal *(n.)* something you are trying to do or achieve

grow up *(v. phr.)* to become an adult

guess *(v.)* to give an answer about something with little or no information

H

health *(n.)* being well; not sick

huge *(adj.)* very large; enormous

I

idea *(n.)* a thought or plan about what to do

imagine *(v.)* to think or create in your mind

impact *(n.)* an effect; a change caused by some action or event

impossible *(adj.)* not able to be done; not possible

improve *(v.)* to make something better

incredible *(adj.)* extremely good; amazing

information *(n.)* facts, details, or knowledge learned about something

inspiration *(n.)* a person, place, or experience that makes someone want to do or create something

interest *(n.)* a feeling of wanting to learn more about something or to be involved in something

invent *(v.)* to make something for the first time

issue *(n.)* an important problem or concern

K

knowledge *(n.)* the information you get from learning about something or from experiencing something

L

lonely *(adj.)* feeling sad because you are alone or not with other people

M

meaning *(n.)* the thing or idea represented by words or gestures

mental *(adj.)* of or relating to the mind (thinking)

messenger *(n.)* someone or something that delivers a message or package

miserable *(adj.)* feeling very unhappy or uncomfortable

modern *(adj.)* of or relating to newer things or ideas

mood *(n.)* the way someone feels

N

negative *(adj.)* relating to bad instead of good

nerves *(n.)* feelings of being worried about something

net *(n.)* a woven fabric used to hold or catch things

normal *(adj.)* ordinary; regular

notice *(v.)* to give attention to; to become aware of something

O

obstacle *(n.)* something that makes it difficult to make progress or move ahead

order *(n.)* a way to arrange things

original *(adj.)* creative; new and different

P

passion *(n.)* a strong feeling of excitement for something

pay attention *(v. phr.)* to listen to, watch, or notice something carefully

peace *(n.)* a quiet, calm state

perform *(v.)* to entertain people: to do an act with great skill

perspective *(n.)* a way of thinking about something

physical *(adj.)* of or relating to the body

pleasure *(n.)* a feeling of being satisfied or happy about something

positive *(adj.)* relating to good instead of bad

presentation *(n.)* an activity where someone explains, describes or shows something to other people

print *(n.)* a mark made on the surface of something; a track

privacy *(n.)* the state of being away from other people

protect *(v.)* to keep someone or something safe; to keep from harm

R

reason *(n.)* a statement that explains why someone acts or thinks a certain way

recognize *(v.)* to know or identify something because you've seen it before

reduce *(v.)* to make something smaller in size, amount, or number

require *(v.)* to need for a special reason

research *(n.)* study that is done to learn or find out about something

respect *(n.)* approval for and thinking highly about the qualities of a person or thing

riddle *(n.)* a question posed as a problem, often with a surprising or funny answer

rule *(n.)* a statement that tells you what you should or should not do

S

save *(v.)* to rescue from danger; to keep safe from harm

seem *(v.)* to appear to be a certain way; to give an appearance that shows a particular feeling or characteristic

selfless *(adj.)* not thinking of oneself; thinking of others first before yourself

shout *(v.)* to say something in a loud voice

smart *(adj.)* controlled by computers and able to do things that seem intelligent

social *(adj.)* liking to talk and be with other people

solution *(n.)* a way of solving a problem

solve *(v.)* to find a way to end a problem; to find the answer

stress *(n.)* a state of worry caused by problems in one's life

style *(n.)* a particular form or design of something

suburbs *(n.)* a smaller town near a bigger city

successful *(adj.)* ending in success; achieving what you want

surprising *(adj.)* causing surprise; unexpected

switch *(v.)* to change around; to replace one with another

T

talented *(adj.)* having a special ability to do something well

task *(n.)* a job; a piece of work to do

tease *(v.)* to laugh at in an unkind way; to make fun of

thoughtful *(adj.)* thinking carefully about something

training *(n.)* a process where someone is taught the skills they need

translate *(v.)* to change words to a different form, like from one language to another

treat *(v.)* to think and act toward someone in a specific way

try *(v.)* to make an attempt to do something

U

unkind *(adj.)* not pleasant; harsh or mean

V

volunteer *(v.)* to freely and willingly offer to do something

W

wander *(v.)* to walk around with no purpose in mind; to move around with no goal

weigh *(v.)* to determine how heavy something is

wild *(adj.)* living in nature with no humans in control

wonder *(v.)* to be interested in knowing or learning something

Y

youth *(n.)* young people, especially teenagers

A

Account A description of facts, conditions, or events.

Adventure story A fiction story that tells about events that are dangerous or exciting. Adventure stories are often fast-paced, have realistic details, include a plot that describes one character having a strong conflict and focuses on suspense. *See also* Suspense

Argument A type of writing or speaking that states the writer's perspective on a topic. Arguments include a claim that is supported by reasons and evidence. *See also* Claim

Argumentative essay An essay that expresses a clear opinion on a question or issue and gives evidence to support that opinion. The purpose is to persuade an audience to agree with the writer's opinion. These essays are often referred to as *argument essays*. *See also* Evidence; Reason

Article A short piece of nonfiction writing that gives facts and information on a specific topic. Articles appear in newspapers and magazines. *See also* Nonfiction; Opinion article; Science article

Autobiography The story of a person's life, written by that person. *See also* Personal narrative

B

Biography The true story of a person's life, written by another person.

C

Caption Text that gives information about something shown visually, such as a photograph. Captions are usually just a few sentences.

Cast of characters A list of all the characters in a play.

Character A person, an animal, or an imaginary creature in a work of fiction. Authors develop characters by showing how the characters grow and change in response to events in the plot.

Characterization The way a writer creates and develops a character. Writers use a variety of ways to bring a character to life: through descriptions of the character's appearance, thoughts, feelings, and actions; through the character's words; and through the words or thoughts of other characters. *See also* Character; Character traits

Character traits The special qualities of personality that writers give their characters. Character traits are revealed through a character's thoughts, words, and actions, and determine how a character responds to events in a story. *See also* Character; Characterization

Chart A type of graphic that includes information, or data, that can be read quickly and easily. Authors use charts to support the information or ideas in the text.

Claim A statement that clearly identifies an author's ideas or opinion. To convince the reader of his or her point of view, the author supports the claim with evidence. *See also* Argument; Evidence

Climax The turning point or most important event in a plot. The climax is often the most exciting event in the story.

Conflict The main problem faced by a character in a story or play. The character may be involved in a struggle against nature, another character, or society. The struggle may also be between two elements in the character's mind. *See also* Rising Action

Connotation The implied meaning of a word or phrase, or what the word makes the readers think and feel. *See also* Denotation

Counterargument The opinion of people who disagree with a claim.

D

Denotation The dictionary meaning of a word or phrase, or literal meaning. *See also* Connotation

Descriptive writing Text that describes a person, place or thing. Descriptive writing creates a picture of the person, place, or thing in the reader's mind.

Diagram A drawing that shows how something looks, how it works, or how it is structured.

Dialogue What characters say to each other.

Drama A story that is performed by actors on a stage. *See also* Play

E

Elevator pitch A short presentation of a business idea. It is short enough that you could explain your idea during an elevator ride.

Epilogue A section or speech at the end of a book, story, or work of drama that functions as a conclusion or comment to what has occurred.

Essay A short piece of nonfiction that discusses a single topic. Its purpose may be to inform, entertain, or persuade. *See also* Argumentative essay; Informational essay; Nonfiction; Problem-solution essay; Topic

Evidence Information provided to support a claim. Evidence provides this support through facts, examples, and statements from experts. *See also* Argument; Claim

Excerpt A part taken out of a longer text.

Exposition The section of a text that introduces the main characters and the setting of the story.

Expository text Text that explains or gives information about a topic.

F

Falling action The actions and events in a plot that happen after the climax. Usually, the major problem is solved in some way, so the remaining events lead to the conclusion of the story.

Fiction Narrative writing about imaginary people, places, things, or events. *See also* Adventure story; Historical fiction; Novel; Realistic fiction; Short story

Figurative language The use of language to express an idea in a way that is different from its common or literal meaning. *See also* Hyperbole; Idiom; Imagery; Literature; Metaphor; Personification; Poetry; Simile; Symbol

First-person point of view A point of view in which one of the characters tells the story. The narrator doesn't know the thoughts and feelings of the other characters. *See also* Narrator; Point of view; Third-person point of view

Free verse Poetry that does not use regular rhyme or rhythm. See Poetry; Rhyme; Rhythm

G

Genre A type or class of literary works grouped according to form, style, and/or topic. Major genres include fictional narrative prose (such as short stories and most novels), nonfiction narrative prose (such as autobiographies, accounts, and biographies), drama, poetry, and the essay. *See also* Essay; Fiction; Literature; Nonfiction; Poetry

Graphic A piece of text that show information visually.

H

Historical fiction Fiction based on events that actually happened or on people who actually lived. However, many of the characters, events, and details are created by the author. It may be written from the point of view of a "real" or an imaginary character, and it usually includes invented dialogue. *See also* Fiction

How-to article An article that explains how to do something. The article contains a list of materials and step-by-step instructions.

Hyperbole Figurative language that exaggerates, often to the point of being funny, to emphasize something. *See also* Figurative language

I

Idiom A phrase or expression that means something different from its dictionary meaning. Idioms cannot be understood literally word for word because an idiom's meaning is not the same as that of the individual words that make it up.

Imagery The use of strong, descriptive details that help readers see or imagine a scene in their minds. Imagery can help the reader imagine how people, places, and things look, sound, taste, smell, and feel. It can also make the reader think about emotions and ideas that commonly go with certain sensations. Because imagery appeals to the senses, it is sometimes called *sensory language*. *See also* Figurative language; Sensory details; Symbol

Infographic A type of graphic that presents information visually with minimal text in the form of labels and captions. *See also* Caption; Label

Informative article An article that presents information in a straightforward manner, without judgment or personal opinion. The author's purpose is to inform.

Informational essay A type of essay in which a writer examines a topic. The writer selects, organizes, and analyzes information to inform the readers about the topic.

Informational report Writing that summarizes key information from an interview, a survey, or a scientific study.

Interview A discussion between two or more people in which questions are asked and answered so that the interviewer can get information. During an interview, someone is usually asked questions about themselves, an area of expertise, or something they are interested in. The record of such a discussion is also called an interview.

J

Journalism The work of gathering and reporting news for newspapers, magazines, radio, television, and other media. *See also* News feature

L

Label A few words that tell readers about what something is. It often has an arrow pointing to what is being labeled.

Letter A written message that is commonly sent between family members, friends, or acquaintances or as a formal exchange with a business or government organization. Letters include a greeting and closing, or sign-off, which appears just before the letter writer's name.

Literature Works written as prose or poetry. *See also* Poetry; Prose

M

Map A picture representation of an area that shows its physical features, such as mountains, streets, and rivers.

Memoir A type of literary nonfiction in which the author writes about experiences from their own lives and often tells what these experiences meant to them. A first-person point of view is used to describe these experiences. Unlike autobiographies, memoirs do not necessarily cover all of the important events in the author's life. *See also* Autobiography, First-person point of view

Metaphor A type of figurative language that compares two unlike things by saying that one thing is the other thing. A metaphor does not use the words *like* or *as* in the comparison. Instead, metaphors often use *be* verbs, such as *is, are, was,* or *were*. *See also* Figurative language; Simile; Symbol

Monologue A long speech in a drama.

Mood The overall feeling or atmosphere a writer creates in a piece of writing.

N

Narrative Writing that gives an account of a set of real or imagined events using descriptive details. Narrative writing includes nonfiction works such as accounts, autobiographies, and biographies, as well as fictional works such as short stories, novels, and plays. *See also* Account; Autobiography; Biography; Fiction; Narrator; Nonfiction; Personal narrative; Play; Plot; Short Story; Story

Narrator Someone who tell what happens in a play. The narrator often gives extra information about the story or characters. *See also* Character

News feature A nonfiction article that gives facts about real people and events. A news feature brings important current information to an audience that wants to be informed about a topic. It should begin with the basic details of the event: who, what, where, when, why, and how. The rest digs deeper with examples and details that bring that basic information to life for the audience. These features are also called *news articles*. *See also* Article; Journalism; Nonfiction

Nonfiction Written works that tell about real events and people and give factual Information. *See also* Autobiography; Biography; Essay; Personal narrative; Report

Novel A long, fictional narrative. Its length enables it to have more characters, a more complicated plot, and a more fully developed setting than shorter works of fiction. Novels are the length of books and are often broken into chapters. *See also* Character; Fiction; Plot; Prose; Setting; Short story.

O

Onomatopoeia The use of words that name the sounds they refer to or describe.

Op-ed Op-ed, short for "opposite the editorial page," is a feature article that expresses the opinion of the author that is not necessarily connected to the newspaper or magazine in which it is printed.

Opinion article Writing where the author argues their viewpoint and tries to convince the reader to think or do something.

Opinion piece Writing where the writer states his or her opinion or beliefs about a specific topic and uses facts, studies, and experts' opinions to persuade readers to agree. *See also* Op-ed; Opinion article

P

Paraphrase A restatement of someone else's ideas in your own words.

Personal narrative A true account of a certain event or set of events in a person's life, written by that person.

Personification A type of figurative language that gives human qualities to animals, objects, and ideas. *See also* Figurative language

Pie chart A type of graph where a circle is divided into sections that represent a portion of the whole.

Play A work of drama, especially one written to be performed on a stage for an audience. *See also* Drama

Plot The series of events and situations in a story or play. Plot is usually divided into five main parts: *exposition, rising action* (or *conflict*), *climax, falling action,* and *resolution*. *See also* Climax; Conflict; Drama; Exposition; Falling action; Resolution; Rising action; Story

Poem A form of literary expression written in lines that can be broken (or ended) where the poet chooses to emphasize words or ideas to create rhyme or rhythm. Poems are written to share an experience or make the reader feel a strong emotion.

Poetry A type of literature that connects to people's thoughts and feelings. *See also* Poem

Point of view The perspective from which the events of a story are told, or narrated. *See also* First-person point of view; Narrator; Third-person point of view

Problem-solution essay A type of essay that explains the importance of an issue. The essay describes the problem and solution with facts, details, and examples and describes the impact of the proposed solution.

Prose A form of writing in which the rhythm is less regular than that of poetry and more like that of ordinary speech. *See also* Poetry; Rhythm

Purpose An author's reason for writing. Most authors write to share personal thoughts or experiences, entertain, explain, inform, describe, or persuade.

R

Realistic fiction Fiction that tells about events that could happen in real life. It includes realistic characters, settings, and plot events. *See also* Fiction

Reason A logical explanation that connects a piece of evidence to a writer or speaker's claim and explains the author's thinking. *See also* Argument; Claim; Evidence

Repetition The repeating of individual vowels and consonants, syllables, words, phrases, lines, or groups of lines. Repetition can be used because it sounds pleasant, to emphasize the words in which it occurs, or to help tie the parts of a text into one structure. *See also* Poetry; Rhyme

Report A usually short piece of nonfiction writing on a particular topic. It differs from an essay in that it normally states only facts and does not directly express the writer's opinions. *See also* Essay; Informational report; Nonfiction; Topic

Resolution The part of a plot that provides details that show how the conflict of a story is solved.

Rhyme The repetition of ending sounds in different words. Rhymes usually come at the end of lines of poems, but they may also occur within a line. *See also* Poem; Poetry; Repetition

Rhythm The natural rise and fall, or "beat," of language. Rhythm is present in all language, including speech and prose, but it is most obvious in poetry. *See also* Poetry; Prose

Rising action The part of a plot that presents actions or events that lead to the climax. These events develop the main character and introduce the conflict. *See also* Conflict

S

Scene A section of text in which there is action and, if there is more than one character, has dialogue. A scene has a beginning, middle, and end and changes when the settings changes, the action ends, or characters arrive or depart.

Science article An article that gives information about a topic having to do with the natural world. It often includes research results, or what scientists learn from what they study. These types of articles will occasionally explain processes and will often contain scientific terms that may be unfamiliar to the non-scientist reader. Science articles are often printed in science journals.

Science fiction A genre of fiction writing that involves story elements that don't exist in the everyday world. It tells a made-up story that is usually set in the future and revolves around some aspect of science and technology, such as space travel, time travel, robots, or aliens invading Earth.

Scientific account Writing in which the author explains scientific ideas to readers who may not be professional scientists.

Script Written directions for dramas, including stage plays and radio plays, that include a list of characters, stage directions, dialogue, and a sequence of scenes. *See also* Dialogue; Stage directions

Sensory details Details that help readers see, feel, hear, smell, and taste what is happening in a text.

Setting The time and location in which the events of a story occur.

Short story A brief, fictional narrative. Like the novel, a short story organizes the action, thought, and dialogue of its characters into a plot. But it tends to focus on fewer characters and to center on a single event. *See also* Character; Fiction; Novel; Plot; Story

Sidebar A boxed text or image of a main text. Writers sometimes include a sidebar to provide additional information about something mentioned in a text. Sidebars can include text features such as bolded text, headings, and bullets.

Simile A type of figurative language that uses the words *like* or as to compare two things.

Skit A short, informal performance that is usually performed by two or more actors. Skits educate, inform, or amuse the audience.

Speech A message on a specific topic that is spoken before an audience.

Stage directions Instructions that tell the actors in a drama how to speak and what to do.

Stanza A group of lines that forms a section of a poem and has the same pattern as other sections of the same poem. In printed poems, stanzas are separated from each other by a space. *See also* Poem

Statistic Numerical data about a topic that can be used as evidence to support a claim. *See also* Claim; Evidence

Story A series of events (actual or imaginary) that can be selected and arranged in a certain order to form a narrative or dramatic plot. *See also* Drama; Plot

Structure The physical form of a type of writing.

Style The way a writer uses language to express the feelings or thoughts they want to convey. Just as no two people are alike, no two styles are exactly alike. A writer's style results from their choices of vocabulary, sentence structure and variety, imagery, figurative language, rhythm, repetition, and other resources.

Suspense A growing sense of curiosity that readers feel about how a story will end.

Symbol A word or phrase that stands for something else, often using figurative language to communicate meaning. *See also* Figurative language

T

Table A graphic that includes information, or data, that can be read quickly and easily. Authors use tables to support the information or ideas in the text.

Theme The message or lesson the author wants the reader to learn. Writers sometimes state the theme directly in a sentence, or readers may need to look more closely at the words the author uses in order to determine the theme.

Timeline A graphic representation of time, such as a chronological arrangement of events in the order of their occurrence or a schedule for when processes will be carried out.

Third-person point of view A point of view in which the story is told by someone who is not in the story. The narrator shares the thoughts and feelings of more than one character. *See also* First-person point of view; Narrator; Point of view

Tone A writer's or speaker's attitude toward his or her topic or subject. A writer's tone may be positive, negative, or neutral. The words the writer chooses, the sentence structure, and the overall pattern of words convey the intended tone. *See also* Connotation; Figurative language; Literature; Mood; Rhythm; Topic

Topic What or who is being discussed in a piece of writing; the subject of the piece. *See also* Theme

V

Viewpoint A character's perspective (what the character sees, feels, and thinks) in a work of fiction. Details that help a reader understand a character's point of view include descriptions of the characters and their feelings, and dialogue. *See also* Point of view

p = picture

Text Credits

UNIT 1

Brave by Svetlana Chmakova © 2017. First published by Yen Press, LLC, New York, NY.

People Are Unhappy, Not Mean by Anna Doherty et al. from Big Ideas for Curious Minds book Reprinted by permission of The School of Life.

UNIT 2

Cao Chong Weighs an Elephant by Pat Betteley from Faces, Jan 2019, Vol. 35 Issue 4 © by Cricket Media, Inc. Reproduced with permission with the following statement: All Cricket Media material is copyrighted by Cricket Media and/or various authors and illustrators. Any commercial use or distribution of material without permission is strictly prohibited. Please visit http://www. cricketmedia.com/info/licensing2 for licensing and http://www.cricketmedia. com for subscriptions.

Youthquake: Youth Involvement in Social Innovation by Judith Lipsett.

UNIT 3

From The Boy And The Whale by Mordicai Gerstein. Copyright © 2017. Reprinted By Permission Of Roaring Brook Press, A Division Of Holtzbrinck Publishing Holdings Limited Partnership. All rights reserved.

The Boy and the Whale by Mordicai Gerstein © 2017 Roaring Book Press. Reprinted with permission from The Marsh Agency, Ltd. With authority from Raines & Raines.

The Subway Experiment by Katherine Catmull. © Cengage Learning 2022.

UNIT 4

Collecting Words by Pat Mora from BOOKJOY WORDJOY. Text Copyright © 2018 by Pat Mora. Permission arranged with LEE & LOW BOOKS, Inc., New York, NY 10016. All rights not specifically granted herein are reserved.

Words are Birds by Francisco X. Alarcón from LAUGHING TOMATOES AND OTHER SPRING POEMS. Text Copyright © 1997 by Francisco X. Alarcón. Permission arranged with Children's Books Press, an imprint of LEE & LOW BOOKS, Inc., New York, NY 10016. All rights not specifically granted herein are reserved.

Forty-Two or Two-and-Forty: Learning Maths in Different Languages. Bahnmueller J, Nuerk H and Cipora K (2020) Forty-Two or Two-and-Forty: Learning Maths in Different Languages. Front. Young Minds. 8:84. doi: 10.3389/frym.2020.00084.

UNIT 5

Material from Hana Hashimoto, Sixth Violin is used by permission of Kids Can Press Ltd., Toronto. Text © 2014 Chieri Uegaki.

Mountain Man of Gelhour by Elizabeth Massie.

UNIT 6

Rickshaw Girl Text copyright © 2007 by Mitali Perkins Illustrations copyright © 2007 by Jamie Hogan Used with permission by Charlesbridge Publishing, Inc. 85 Main Street Watertown, MA 02472 (617) 926-0329 www. charlesbridge.com. All rights reserved.

Amalia Hernández: A Dancer's Dream by Jane Skinner.

UNIT 7

The Peace of Wild Things by Wendell Berry from New Collected Poems. Copyright © 2012 by Wendell Berry. Reprinted with the permission of The Permissions Company, LLC on behalf of Counterpoint Press, counterpointpress. com.

I Wandered Lonely as a Cloud by William Wordsworth from the Book of Nature Poetry: More than 200 Poems with Photographs That Float, Zoom, and Bloom! (National Geographic).

Why We Need Nature by Katie Parker.

UNIT 8

Excerpt(s) from EAGER by Helen Fox, copyright © 2004 by Helen Fox. Used by permission of Wendy Lamb Books, an imprint of Random House Children's Books, a division of Penguin Random House LLC. All rights reserved.

Excerpt(s) from EAGER. Reproduced by permission of Hodder Children's Books, an imprint of Hachette Children's Books, Carmelite House, 50 Victoria Embankment, London imprint, EC4Y 0DZ.

The Queen of the Curve by Wafa' Tarnowska. Zaha Hadid from Amazing Women of the Middle East: 25 Stories from Ancient Times to Present Day. Copyright © 2020 Interlink Publishing Group. Reprinted by permission of 2020 Interlink Publishing Group.

Illustrator Credits

UNIT 2 Cao Chong Weighs an Elephant, Rudy Farber.

UNIT 3 The Boy and Whale, Gemma Capdevi.

UNIT 5 Hana Hashimoto, Sixth Violin, Kelsey Garrity Riley.

UNIT 5 The Mountain Man Gehlour, Borris Stolov.

UNIT 6 Rickshaw Girl, Albert Espi.

UNIT 8 Smart House, Igor Ivanova.

Photographic Credits

COVER: Visual China Group via Getty Images/Visual China Group via Getty Images

UNIT 1

2–3 ©NurPhoto/Getty Images. 6 (tl) ©HRAUN/E+/Getty Images, (tr) ©Gorodenkoff/Shutterstock. com, (cl) ©David Tiberio/Alamy, (cr) ©Ryuhei Shindo/Digital Vision/Getty Images, (bl) ©SeventyFour/iStock/ Getty Images Plus, (br) ©Courtney Hale/E+/Getty Images. 7 ©George Frey/Getty Image News/Getty Images. 28–29 ©Courtesy of Brent Stirton. 29 (br) ©Courtesy of Brent Stirton. 30 (tl) ©SDI Productions/Getty Images, (tr) antoniodiaz/Shutterstock.com, (cl) ©MBI/Alamy, (cr) ©Monkey Business Images/Shutterstock.com, (bl) ©HBRH/ Shutterstock.com, (br) ©SolStock/E+/ Getty Images. 32 Phil Boorman/Image Source/Getty Images. 34 ©gawrav/E+/ Getty Images. 38 ©Souvvant/AFP/Getty Images. 39 (l) ©imageBROKER/Alamy, (r) Winfried Wisniewski/The Image Bank/Getty Images. 43 ©Anadolu/ Anadolu Agency/Getty Images. 46 (t) ©Hannah Reyes Morales/National Geographic Image Collection, (b) ©Hannah Reyes Morales/National Geographic Image Collection.

UNIT 2

48–49 ©Matt Nager/Redux. 52 (tl) ©amanda rose/Alamy, (tr) ©Rido/ Shutterstock.com, (cl) ©John Scott/The Image Bank/Getty Images, (cr) ©Sekar B/ Shutterstock.com, (bl) ©Zoonar GmbH/ Alamy, (br) ©sizovin/iStock/Getty Images. 54 ©Rich Carey/Shutterstock.